SELMA EVANS

NARCISSISTIC MOTHERS

Quiet the Critical Voice in Your Head and
Rewrite Your Story After Emotional Abuse

ISBN: 979-12-81498-35-8

TABLE OF CONTENTS

INTRODUCTION

Being a child requires us to look to our parents for love, support, and encouragement. Our parents lay the groundwork for feelings of security and confidence in others. As children grow older, it is critical for them to feel seen and heard by their loved ones. Growing up with a parent who denies a child these emotional security blankets can be extremely painful. This is, unfortunately, the reality for children raised by narcissistic mothers.

Our narcissistic mothers were incapable of loving us the way we needed to be loved. Their self-absorption left no room for the needs of their children. Many of us grew up feeling invisible, and this lack of validation has stayed with us throughout our lives. This can result in the sense that we are unimportant and unlovable.

Unfortunately, many of us grew up deeply ashamed and with a deep sense that something was fundamentally wrong with us. We may feel that our very being is unworthy and flawed. We may go through life feeling like no one will love or accept us as we are

– unless we become more perfect or somehow more complete than we already are.

One of the things that is so difficult about being in this position is that we can't see how our parents are responsible for our pain. It's like living inside a nightmare and believing that we are powerless to change it. We may go through life feeling like we are fundamentally flawed, unable to please others or keep them happy, and worthless.

We may be turning to other people for love, and sometimes, despite our best efforts, we may find the love that others offer us disappointing at best and intolerable at worst.

We all know perfectly healthy and happy people – yet they are not known for their charm or brightness. And yet some always seem to do well for themselves and in life. They're attractive and competent, and they've attracted a partner or a circle of friends that makes them look even more successful. They are often quite charming and witty, well-liked by others, and highly regarded.

At the same time, these people often have siblings whose lives seem to be absolute disasters – they're struggling with personal relationships and work; they lack any self-confidence or even self-esteem. Many of them seem to act like failures even when they've done nothing wrong – but some relatively innocent act from someone around them seems to cause a destructive reaction.

We may feel like these two groups of people are worlds apart – but how can they be? How are these two groups so different despite being raised by the same parents? Further, why do some of us have such an uphill struggle in life, while others seem to have an easy time of it?

We may be tempted to leave our mothers out of the equation because their behavior seems to be so far removed from our experience. We may not yet have seen this side of them – and for those who haven't, it isn't easy to imagine it. However, once we have caught a glimpse, it's easy to see the truth of the matter. No matter how much they may deny it, our mothers are narcissists – and they are not interested in our happiness or well-being.

It is a problem that we are usually not aware of narcissistic tendencies until we're adults. This is one of the problems with narcissistic mothers; we were too young to see that there was anything wrong with them as parents – thus, it took great pressure from other people to make us realize that something was amiss.

It is said that children know the difference between love and abuse before they even understand what "love" means. To understand what narcissistic mothers are like, we must understand how they behave.

Our mothers have an insatiable need to be the center of attention, approval, and admiration. They are rarely satisfied with how they live their lives – they want more. They make up stories about other people and themselves to feel unique and special. They look to others for admiration – and if someone doesn't admire them enough, or at all, then they believe something is wrong or missing with them or their life choices.

People who have narcissistic mothers tend to become attracted to others who have selfish family members in their lives – those whose lives match their own. These people don't want to be with anyone who isn't self-absorbed – after all, it's impossible to love and be loved by someone who doesn't love or care about themselves.

Many of us have had an experience of being rejected by someone we love, thinking that if only they loved us back in the same way, we would be happy. We may feel that we can't survive without those kinds of assurances from other people – it's the only way to feel worthwhile and worth loving. We may cling to people who could never meet our needs because giving up is too painful and scary.

We may feel like we don't know how to love other people because we have been so deeply hurt as children it seems impossible to trust anyone again. We may be afraid of loving other people because we believe that they will inevitably hurt us in the same way. We may even have become accustomed to being in pain – and we fear that if we let ourselves love someone else, they will take our sense of self away just as our narcissistic mothers did.

CHAPTER 1: WHAT IS NARCISISTIC PERSONALITY DISORDERS (NPD)?

Narcissistic Personality Disorder is an excessively narcissistic or self-involved pattern of behavior, thought processes, and social interaction. Narcissists have a sense of grandiosity, lack empathy, and have a sense of entitlement. They are unable to accept responsibility for their deeds, their actions are often "done to them," and they need to maintain an image of perfection to boost their self-esteem. An inflated sense of self-importance characterizes Narcissistic Personality Disorder, often combined with a belief in one's specialness or uniqueness. Narcissists are highly manipulative, using many of the charm tactics used by psychopaths. Females suffer more than males with the disorder because they are more likely to internalize their false sense of grandiosity and their self-obsession. The "Golden Child Syndrome" has been coined to explain the narcissistic mother's behavior, which can be far more damaging than a child who exhibits normal sibling rivalry. Many therapists have found the treatment of Narcissistic Personality Disorder extremely difficult because they fail to identify the symptoms early on, thus allowing the narcissist to gain control over their victims. Narcissists do not always present themselves as self-serving because they have a strong sense of entitlement and believe that their actions can only benefit others.

A narcissist is moderately or severely dysfunctional in their personality, which means they have delicate and dysfunctional self-esteem, very low tolerance for criticism, an excessive need for admiration, and a lack of ability to empathize with others. Narcissists admire those they perceive as having high status or power. They feel highly threatened by people with more power or higher status than themselves; for example, if their spouse has been promoted at work and the narcissist has been demoted, the narcissist will feel threatened and possibly insecure. When confronted with a superior who is more powerful than they are, the narcissist will attempt to manipulate or control the individual with their false sense of grandiosity or omnipotence. Sometimes, narcissists might not present themselves as self-serving, even when using others to attain power because they have a strong sense of entitlement and believe that their actions can only benefit others. Low self-esteem, poor self-concept, and low self-confidence disguise their true nature. Narcissists are often very charismatic and intelligent in social situations but are often unable to perform the work of real life. They lack emotional maturity and the drive to improve themselves, so they have no insight into their emotional problems.

Narcissists have shallow affective empathy; they do not understand other people's feelings well or accurately, especially feelings of guilt or shame. They tend to be intolerant of criticism and frequently blame others for problems that they themselves create. Narcissists have a chronic sense of entitlement. They expect others to cater to them, so they are often disappointed when others disregard their needs. Narcissism is a self-serving disorder, and the narcissist will not admit that the criticism was deserved or that they were at fault. Narcissists have a distorted sense of reality and are very self-centered. They often make grandiose claims and expect others to validate them as right or special. They are likely to be highly adulated by groups but will easily criticize others or be callous toward them if they fail to provide the expected positive attention.

What is Healthy Narcissism?

A narcissistic mother can be wonderful when she is realistic about her strengths and achievements, balances them with her weaknesses, takes responsibility for her actions, and allows other people to help her. Genuine admiration and encouragement can be extremely helpful to any mother; the goal of healthy narcissism is to nurture a real person with regard to her strengths and weaknesses, and encourage her to take responsibility for her actions, and help others. Healthy narcissism does not lead to extreme arrogance, or arrogance at all.

A healthy narcissistic mother is not self-obsessed and does not blame her failures on others. She tries to encourage her children to have the same self-esteem as she does, teaching them that they must try hard in life, be sensitive toward others, and have empathy.

Healthy narcissism is also about having empathy, which is defined as the ability to be sensitive and responsive to other people's needs and feelings, and the ability to imagine what another person is feeling. Empathy is extremely important in the family unit because when one person empathizes with another, they can better understand them.

Narcissistic mothers, just like all other human beings, can be very loving, sensitive, and caring toward their children. They can also be very punishing if they feel their children have failed them or let them down. Narcissistic mothers are often overprotective of their children because they do not want their children to fail, but they can also be extremely harsh when their children do not meet their expectations.

The love of one's parents is the most important thing in a child's life. However, many narcissistic mothers overemphasize the importance of their children's admiration and affection over independent thinking and competence. Narcissistic mothers are more likely to promote co-dependency than independent thinking, which can cause emotional damage to children in adulthood.

Narcissistic mothers spend a great deal of time and energy thinking about their looks and social status. They place a premium on how others perceive them and their appearance. This can lead them to be preoccupied with how successful they are, what other people think about them, or how popular they are. Healthy narcissism is not about preoccupation with how others perceive them, but rather it's about having a healthy concern for their self-image.

Healthy narcissism does not involve any sense of superiority or grandiosity. It promotes humility so that the person can be aware of their strengths and weaknesses.

Narcissistic mothers can be very aware of what others are thinking and feeling, so as to make sure they meet the expectations they have created in themselves. Hypercritical parents often use denial to avoid their inability to meet those unrealistic expectations. Conversely, healthy narcissists are aware of their flaws, and strive to improve themselves accordingly.

CHAPTER 2: DIFFERENT TYPES OF NARCISSISM

Narcissistic Personality Disorder is the name of the condition given to a person with an inflated sense of self-importance, an intense need for admiration and validation, and a lack of empathy. Children with narcissistic parents are at risk for emotional problems like depression. They often have low self-esteem and experience shame, which impairs their development by hampering healthy boundaries.

Narcissistic mothers are not always aware of the importance of their behavior in shaping the emotional lives of their children. Their lack of self-awareness may be destructive in the long term, as they do not understand how their behaviors affect those around them.

A mother with Narcissistic Personality Disorder might not be aware that she is undermining her children's sense of self-worth or causing them to feel embarrassed and inadequate. This can lead to depression, anxiety, and other forms of mental illness.

Different Types of Narcissism

Exhibitionist Type

Exhibitionist narcissists are extroverted, charming, and engaging. They love the admiration of others and thrive on positive feedback. Their concern is to look good in the eyes of others and seek constant validation for their self-worth. Narcissistic mothers may seem confident and secure but often feel weak and vulnerable underneath it all. They cannot handle discomfort and have a low tolerance for pain or emotional distress. This kind of narcissism is associated with a lack of empathy for other people's feelings, which leads to manipulative behavior to get their needs met. You can see these types of characteristics in many narcissistic mothers.

Mothers with exhibitionist narcissism tend to be very controlling and manipulative. They can also be very critical of their children, which causes the children to have low self-esteem.

Mothers who suffer from this type of narcissism will make you feel like it is your fault they are upset or mad at you. They tend to get so carried away with themselves that they can't see that anything else matters other than their opinion or needs.

This kind of mother will come off as "too good" for anyone else, sometimes seeming prideful and cocky. These mothers are often materialistic, taking great pride in their possessions and belongings.

Mothers that are narcissists of this type can usually be found in leadership positions due to their confidence and knack for self-promotion. They like being in charge of things and often have natural leadership abilities.

Mothers that are exhibitionist narcissists tend to see their children as extensions of themselves, or objects. This leads them to be emotionally detached from their children and emotionally manipulative.

Mothers with this form of narcissism tend to see people as a reflection of themselves, making them very judgmental and critical. This attitude is apparent when these mothers interact with their children. Exhibitionist narcissistic mothers will often control how you dress, who you hang out with, and what you do for fun. Emotional abuse can be caused by:

- Being highly critical and insulting

- Telling you that your choices are worthless or "no good"

- Making remarks about your weight or physical appearance: "You look like a pig in that dress"

- Explaining why it's "not enough" and telling you that

you need to try harder

- Having unrealistic expectations of you

- Throwing a fit if something is not done as they want

Mothers with exhibitionist narcissism are often "mean girls" in high school who make you feel like being friends with or associating with them is a mistake. These mothers tend to be very rude and act superior, which makes others resent them, yet they never seem to notice or care that they hurt people with their behavior.

Mothers who exhibit this type of narcissism will often use their children's accomplishments to make themselves look better. This is called grandiose exhibitionism. They may brag about their children excessively, almost as if they are bragging about themselves. Similarly, narcissistic mothers will often be very critical of their children, which causes them to have low self-worth and little self-esteem.

Mothers with this kind of narcissism usually feel like other people don't matter, unless they can offer something to the narcissist herself.

Grandiose Narcissism

This type of narcissism is influenced by parental behavior. If the parent is demanding, critical, and critical of the child's efforts, they may grow up thinking they are less than everyone else and a failure. A grandiose narcissist will have a strong desire to be admired and loved by others without feeling deserving. They also may feel vulnerable in their relationships. Children of these narcissists can also experience low self-esteem and an intense need to be validated by the people in their lives because they feel worthless and unimportant. They are not so concerned with getting attention and admiration from other people; rather, they want to feel valuable, respected, and important.

Mothers with this type of narcissism will be very critical of their children and not give them the attention or admiration they need.

Mothers who suffer from grandiose narcissism feel like they have an extreme lack of control over their lives. They have a tendency to see other people as inanimate objects with no personality or thoughts. They may come off as arrogant and judgmental, especially when you explain things to them.

Mothers who exhibit grandiose narcissism tend to be highly critical of their children and friends. They also tend to be critical of people outside of their immediate relationships, making it difficult for them to make friends or get close to anyone.

Mothers who suffer from this type of narcissism will seldom praise you for anything. They will never seem to care about your opinions or needs. This can make you feel inept or incompetent, as if no matter what you do, you will never be good enough. These mothers tend to make others feel bad about themselves and can come off as unapproachable.

Mothers who are grandiose narcissistic typically were the "popular" people in high school or the type that believed "you're either with us or against us." They may set these kinds of examples in their lives where they don't let anyone get close to them – always keeping friends at arm's length. These mothers don't seem to notice that they hurt people with their behavior, which can cause others to resent them.

Grandiose narcissists are preoccupied with the opinion that others have of them. This abuse can create insecurity in their child, which will cause them to grow up feeling like they are not equal to anyone else. Without receiving praise and recognition, these children can develop a need for other people's validation because they don't feel valued or worthy of love, causing them to be very insecure about themselves and their abilities.

Mothers who exhibit grandiose narcissism can be cold and not show much affection for their children. They may seem distant and not interested in what you have to say. They may have an intense need for attention from other people and admiration from the people they care about. If they feel like they don't get enough attention from you or anyone else, they may become very angry or behave in a very mean or hurtful way towards you.

They may also become very indignant if anyone challenges their beliefs or opinions.

The grandiose narcissistic mothers will often make decisions for their children because they think they know what is best. They may not give the child a chance to voice an opinion or make their own decisions, which can cause the child to feel disrespected. These mothers may feel a lack of control in their lives and decide to take it out on people around them.

Mothers who have grandiose narcissism will have a great time getting others to admire them and validate their existence. They may have a great time telling others about their interests and achievements, but they will not listen to what other people think about these things, making the people around them feel disrespected.

Grandiose narcissistic mothers tend to struggle with low self-esteem and may become very angry or upset when they do not receive approval from others.

This narcissism is related to poor parenting practices, parental overindulgence, and parental neglect. It can create mother-child relationship problems where the parent uses guilt and manipulation to get what they want instead of showing praise, guidance, and interest in their children's lives. This kind of narcissistic abuse can harm a child's self-esteem as they grow older because they are always told that nothing they do will never be good enough. This type of narcissistic abuse can cause the child to become overly anxious because they never seem to be able please their parents, no matter how hard they try.

Mothers who suffer from this kind of narcissism will often use their children as their toys. They may use guilt and manipulation to get what they want from their children, instead of respecting them or showing interest in what they have to say or do.

Mothers who have grandiose narcissism will have a hard time knowing how others feel about them. They may also have impaired empathy because they don't feel that others are as important as themselves.

Malignant Type

Malignant narcissists lack the skills to get their needs met through healthy means. They will resort to manipulation, aggression, intimidation, and violence to get what they want. Malignant narcissism stems from a deep sense of insecurity and vulnerability. It is caused by feeling powerless, weak, and worthless as a child. This type of narcissism may arise because a child was outraged at any form of abuse by their caregivers when they were young. They may have experienced neglect, been treated poorly, over-burdened with chores, and made to care for themselves, causing them to feel powerless and worthless. They may have also experienced harsh punishment for their mistakes, causing them to feel like they could never do anything right.

Mothers with this kind of narcissism may have difficulty accepting their feelings and emotions. They may begin to feel angry and bitter towards other people because they feel like others are taking advantage of them.

Mothers who suffer from this type of narcissism can be very violent towards others because they are often angry at how life has treated them. They will often lash out when things don't go their way, causing others to fear having anything to do with them. Her children may suffer some abuse from their mother, causing them to feel uncomfortable around her.

Malignant narcissistic mothers lack the skills needed to be a good parent because they are so caught up in their problems and thoughts. They cannot meet their child's needs because of their low self-esteem, self-hatred, and feelings of worthlessness.

Mothers with this kind of narcissism will often resort to aggression or violence when they don't get what they want. They may also lash out at others when they feel like they are not being treated right or their needs are not being met.

The child cannot help but feel worried or afraid of the mother who is angry and aggressive towards them because she may lash out at them verbally or even physically abuse them in some cases.

The child does not know how to deal with this type of behavior, so they may avoid the mother, which causes further damage to their self-esteem.

The Covert Type

Covert narcissists can hide their true nature from their significant others. Some experts believe that covert narcissism is an indirect version of Narcissistic Personality Disorder. This condition can be very harmful to children as they are not likely to receive validation or love from their parents, making them feel like failures in life.

Some experts believe that covert narcissism is a more socially acceptable form of narcissism because those with the condition may present themselves as friendly, caring, and compassionate people who want to make their friends and family happy. Covert narcissists can also take on other personality types or behaviors to hide their feelings about themselves and others.

The covert narcissist has a deep need for attention, but does not want to be criticized by others for how they behave or what they think, causing them to repress their true nature from others. Mothers who have this kind of narcissism are often very upset and disturbed by everyone around them. They may feel angry and confused about the people they interact with, making it hard to know what they want or need. They would rather express their needs to others instead of asking for help or input because it would make them feel bad about themselves.

The covert narcissist will avoid several indicators that cause others to know that they have a narcissistic personality disorder. A mother may refuse to acknowledge her own needs, her feelings, or the feelings of others. She will deny any problems she may have, causing others to believe that everything is all right when it isn't.

Mothers with covert narcissism will attempt to alter their behavior in order to conceal their true selves from others. She will try not to show her true intentions when she is with other people, sometimes even telling lies about herself or what she thinks or feels. The child may wish to please the mother, who is very critical of them and their actions, causing them to feel like they have to change who they are for other people.

The covert narcissist may also feel uncomfortable with compliments or praise from others.

However, the covert narcissist is very self-centered and has a strong sense of entitlement because they feel as though they are better than everyone else. They are also very smart, cunning, and manipulative.

The covert narcissist is very critical of others, making it difficult for them to have positive relationships or get close with others.

They may also have abandonment issues and be prone to inappropriate sexual behavior.

The Abusive Type

Individuals who suffer from this type of narcissism may feel very restless and confused about who they are as people. They may also feel like they can never do anything right because they are always under scrutiny or judgment by others. The abusive narcissist has a deep need for control and being right, which causes them to lash out at those who do not agree with their point of view. The children of these mothers are often raised in an abusive environment, which can cause them to develop a risk appetite for abuse and violence.

Some experts believe that abusive narcissism is a form of covert narcissism because sufferers do not want others to know about their true nature. They may try to hide their needs and emotions from the people around them and do what they can to avoid being criticized by those they care about.

Abusive narcissists will often hate the people in their lives, mistreating them or humiliating them.

The abusive narcissist will also feel uncomfortable when she is around other people. She may worry about what others think about her and feel ashamed of who she is as a person. She may also have trouble forming healthy relationships with others because she feels as though she is better than everyone.

The abusive narcissist has a strong need to control everything around her and have power over those around her. She will show her anger and frustration by using physical or emotional abuse on the people in her life. The mother with this type of personality disorder will punish her children if they do not follow her rules, causing them to develop a lack of trust in the relationship.

The abusive narcissist is very ashamed of who she is and what others think about her. She will try to change or alter her behavior or appearance to please other people to get them to like her or accept her. She will avoid several indicators that cause others to know she has a Narcissistic Personality Disorder. She may refuse to acknowledge her own needs, feelings, or the feelings of those around her, making it hard for friends and family members to know what they want or need. She will deny any problems she may have, causing others to believe that everything is all right when it isn't.

The abusive narcissist wants to control everything around them and be right about everything in their lives. They will punish people if they do not agree with what they say or believe, causing the child of an abusive narcissistic parent to become afraid of the person they love the most.

The Hypervigilant Type

This type of narcissism is characterized by chronic insecurity and constant validation. People with hypervigilant narcissism are hypersensitive to the criticism of others, even when it is not intended.

Hypervigilant narcissists tend to be controlling in their relationships. This stems from their desire to manipulate others into feeling responsible for them. They also tend to be hypersensitive to comments directed at them and make mountains out of molehills. This stems from their deep-seated belief that they are not worthy of the love and praise that others give them. Because this type of narcissism is multi-faceted and complex, it isn't easy for sufferers to get the help they need. Mothers with this type of narcissism can often be emotionally unavailable to their children.

Mothers with hypervigilant narcissism may use blame, shame, and guilt to manipulate what other people think about them. They may also try to control their kids or other relationships or even treat themselves badly to feel better than others. They may also be very critical of how other people behave around them and react negatively to certain words or actions.

Mothers with this kind of narcissism may also have problems with self-esteem and may try to overcompensate, so people think they are more than they truly are. Mothers with hypervigilant narcissism may also be prone to abuse their partners or children for attention and manipulation.

Children of mothers with this type of narcissism may grow up having a distorted view of themselves and others. They may also form unhealthy relationships and struggle with intimacy, trust, rejection, and feeling worthy or loved. They may have trouble getting close to others, for fear of being hurt or abandoned. The child of an hypervigilant narcissist can often experience emotional abuse or neglect from their mothers, making it harder for them to develop normal emotional bonds with other people.

Children of hypervigilant narcissists are often confused about what they want in life because they are taught that wanting something is selfish. They can also feel like they need to be perfect or change who they are for other people. Being raised by a hypervigilant narcissist can also cause children to have issues around self-esteem, confidence, and interpersonal relationships.

The Oblivious Type

The oblivious narcissist is a common form of narcissism that stems from abuse or neglect. Since sufferers were not raised in a nurturing environment, they do not interact with others effectively and often feel alienated. This type of narcissism can lead to isolation and a lack of self-help skills because individuals find it hard to trust others. They are very timid and do not understand why anyone would want to be around them. It may seem like they are more interested in being alone than having a relationship with anyone else. They also feel like people are trying to hurt them.

The oblivious narcissist will often feel abandoned and alone, and as though they cannot survive without their significant other. They can become depressed, anxious, or have low self-esteem due, and blame themselves for being rejected.

Children of mothers with oblivious narcissism may grow up with poor self-esteem, lack of emotional connection, and problems trusting others. They may also try to control things around them because they do not have the skills to cope with their problems or be in charge of anything. They may also have issues with anxiety and depression, which may cause them to turn to drugs or alcohol, or other unhealthy coping mechanisms.

Children of mothers with this type of narcissism are often bullied or mistreated by their peers, resulting in low self-esteem. Children of mothers with this type of narcissism often struggle to trust others because they have been taught that everyone is out to get them.

The Shallow Type

People with shallow narcissism cannot empathize with other people and lack a sense of self-worth. They cannot make decisions based on long-term consequences and instead place a high value on instant gratification. They use shallow tactics to get what they want and are unaware of how they affect others, making it difficult to make positive changes in their relationships.

An example of a shallow narcissist would be a person who is easily angered or upset based on little to no provocation. They tend to talk negatively about others behind their back and have bad attitudes, feelings, and perspectives on life. They often put themselves first by manipulating the people and situations around them. Mothers with this kind of narcissism can be very vindictive and treat their children poorly. They may use them to manipulate other people or take revenge on their partners for whatever reason. They often have issues with trust, thinking others will betray them. Mothers with this type of narcissism often have low self-esteem, self-hatred, and lack a sense of purpose in life.

Children of mothers with this type of narcissism can struggle emotionally, have trust issues, or be unwilling to share things about themselves for fear of being rejected. They may grow up feeling unloved and unwanted because such an absent parent raised them.

The children of mothers with this type of narcissism may suffer from depression or anxiety, affecting the way they live their lives in the present. They also may have trouble forming close, long-lasting relationships because they fear being betrayed or mistreated. Additionally, there is a strong likelihood that they will also grow up to be narcissistic as a result of the way they were raised.

The Compulsive Type

People with this type of narcissism often have a great sense of superiority and entitlement, making them seem very self-absorbed. They do everything possible to fulfill their needs and are very competitive in order to gain the upper hand in any situation. They tend to be bad listeners and do not know how to respond appropriately or interact with others.

A mother who has this type of narcissism would get involved in many activities but never seem content. She may collect useless or unnecessary things, and have many different hobbies or collections, but never makes any progress. She also tends to make unhealthy or dangerous lifestyle choices.

Children of mothers with this type of narcissism may seem like they have an extroverted personality but may not be comfortable in social settings because they are unaware of how to behave. They tend to act negatively around other people, making it hard to find friends or make connections in life. They can also get upset easily when they do not get their way. Children with mothers who have this type of narcissism may grow up without a sense of motivation and attempt risky behaviors like drugs, alcohol, and unprotected sex.

Since their mother could not help them form self-esteem, they develop a sense of self-loathing or guilt. This can also lead to depression, anxiety, and other issues.

The Pathological Type

People with this type of narcissism are the most extreme or self-absorbed of all. They have trouble empathizing with others and often believe they are above the law. They can be very aggressive, if not violent, towards others to get what they want, and expect things because they believe they deserve it.

A mother who has this type of narcissism does not care about anyone else except herself. She may become offended if someone does something for her, like opening a door or helping her move, and sometimes does not accept help when it is offered.

Children of mothers with this type of narcissism grow up without boundaries and can seem very spoiled. They have a hard time empathizing with other people, seeing themselves as the center of the universe. They lack many feelings, especially guilt or empathy, and can be disrespectful towards others. They also tend to be very impatient and expect things to happen immediately for them. Additionally, they may struggle with depression, anxiety, and other problems.

The Stealth Narcissist

Some narcissistic mothers cannot be categorized as any of the types above. They may seem like loving, caring parents but have very manipulative personalities. These are the most covert type of narcissists. The stealth narcissist is hard to identify because they seem so compassionate and loving to their children in public. However, when they are not around other people, they make their children feel unwanted or worthless. They may also make their children feel that others cannot be trusted or that there is something wrong with them for feeling as if something is wrong.

The stealth narcissistic mother often does not have a lot of friends and has trouble forming intimate connections with others unless she gets something out of it herself. She may demand sympathy from others and feel like she is a victim in life. She will often get involved with other people's lives and end up doing too much to help them without being asked, even though they are not her responsibility.

Children of a stealth narcissistic mother may avoid social situations, thinking all people are out to get them or that they cannot trust anyone. This makes it difficult for them to develop friendships or relationships. They also have low self-esteem and feel they have done something wrong, no matter what they do.

A mother who has this covert narcissist disorder will often do things for her children, making them feel like their lives are her responsibility and that they owe her because she helps them. She might even use guilt trips to get what she thinks she deserves. This can make the children of a stealth narcissistic mother feel as if they have to work extra hard to accomplish anything in their lives, and that they must always be there for their mother, even when they would rather be doing something else.

The Vulnerable Narcissist

Vulnerable narcissists can be very caring and kind to their children but have a hard time handling criticism from others or believing they have done something wrong. They will often make excuses for themselves instead of facing problems.

They may also expect things to turn out well for them in life, even though they may not work as hard as other people. Because of this, they feel like others should give them things, and everything should be handed to them because they are special. This can make dealing with failure, rejection, or criticism more difficult for them. They may not express their feelings of hurt and anger because they believe it makes them look bad in front of others.

Children of this type of mother may not trust other people because their mother did not trust them. Because their mother always wanted to be the best, she would make her children feel like there was something wrong with them for not excelling at everything in life, and that they had to be perfect for her to love them.

They may also feel that no one cares about them or could ever understand how they feel because their parents never cared about them enough or listened to what they had going on in their lives.

The Inverted Narcissist

This type of narcissism can be difficult to detect. A person with this disorder may be very supportive and caring at first but will stop caring about other people's feelings or may even tease others or use sarcasm when situations call for it.

Those with this type of narcissism tend to be very high-functioning in society and may be seen as model parents. They frequently go to any length to obtain what they desire and are generally indifferent to the feelings of others. If a child does something wrong, the parent will say, "It does not matter to me" or, "I couldn't care less."

Their children often feel used or unappreciated, and like their parents do not love them. They may also have low self-esteem because they never felt worth anything to their mom in the first place.

Differentiating between Negative and Healthy Narcissism

The essence of healthy narcissism is the capacity for self- and other love. Thus, it lacks the desire to exploit and harm others that characterize Narcissistic Personality Disorder, in which love is exclusively self-directed. In its initial years, child-parent relationships can be used to illustrate healthy narcissism. A parent who showers the child with affection and attention, and is sensitive and attuned to the child's needs for comfort and nurturance, shows healthy narcissism. Negative narcissism in all its manifestations involves a distorted view of the self and the world and may lead to behaviors that harm others. The adult who pays attention only to a preferred few and is insensitive to the needs of the many in his own family, community, or nation is a classic example of a negative narcissist. In the most extreme form of negative narcissism, one can find the sadistic narcissist.

According to the current literature, there are three types of healthy narcissism:

1. Realistic/Adaptive Narcissism

This represents realistic confidence and self-esteem based on solid achievements, high self-efficacy, social recognition, and genuine competence. It is not inflated, grandiose or fragile. It is based on legitimate grounds, and the individual can cope well with setbacks, criticism, and negative feedback. The realistic type of healthy narcissism is similar to ego-strength, described by A. H. Maslow as distinguishing between healthy and unhealthy levels of self-esteem or self-confidence. The individual possesses a strong sense of identity, agency, purpose, competence, and autonomy.

2. Compensatory Narcissism

This type of narcissism develops as a reaction to early trauma or abuse. It represents an attempt by the individual to protect himself from further abuse and to maintain a sense of power and self-esteem. This type of narcissism is not ego-syntonic (i.e., it is not enjoyed by the individual) but compensatory (i.e., a defense mechanism aimed at surviving harsh reality). It manifests itself in reactions of rage, shame, envy, and possibly aggression triggered by any sign of contempt or devaluation from others. It is a fragile form of narcissism and can easily be upset. This type of narcissism is based on fantasies of grandeur and "specialness," which can deteriorate into delusions of inflated self-importance or full-fledged personality disorders.

3. Grandiose Narcissism

This is the classical, flamboyant, exhibitionistic narcissism, a gross exaggeration of the real self. It is characterized by fantasies of unlimited success, power, brilliance, beauty, or ideal love. Individuals with grandiose narcissism believe that they are "special" and unique and can only be understood by other special/superior people. Special rights and entitlements usually accompany these fantasies. When the person with exquisite narcissistic traits interacts with others, he typically expects to be recognized as superior without commensurate achievements.

It is important to differentiate between these types of narcissism to adequately understand the specific nature of an individual's condition. This differentiation allows the clinician to assess the severity of pathological narcissism and determine the relative contribution of environmental and genetic factors in developing and maintaining a Narcissistic Personality Disorder.

CHAPTER 3: THE NARCISSISTIC SPECTRUM DISORDER AND STATISTICS

About 1% of the adult population has a Narcissistic Personality Disorder (NPD). While narcissistic personality disorder is present in all age groups, the incidence peaks between 10 and 14 years when children's personal needs and moods are most easily influenced. Although it is common for narcissists to reach their 40s and 50s before being diagnosed, on average, it takes 20 years from the onset of symptoms to receive a diagnosis. Even though NPD is a relatively common disorder, few narcissists ever seek therapy. Although many narcissists lack the insight to see they have a problem, they usually recognize that their behavior is unacceptable to others.

Men tend to exhibit more narcissistic traits than women, although NPD is diagnosed more frequently in women than in men. People of all cultures and ethnicities are affected by NPD.

The prevalence of pathological narcissism in the general population is estimated at 1%-2%.

There is no known racial or ethnic predisposition, nor any socio-cultural background which makes one group more vulnerable than another to develop a narcissistic personality structure, though studies indicate that there might be a greater incidence of NPD in urban areas versus rural areas.

NPD symptoms vary with each individual, but most people eventually improve after treatment. However, 16% (1 in 6) continue to exhibit some narcissistic features up to the time they die.

Most people with NPD react poorly to criticism. They are more likely to respond with counterattacks and excuses rather than accept responsibility for the criticism.

Narcissistic Personality Disorder is generally considered a chronic condition that fluctuates over time. Most people do not change much their entire lives, but children of narcissistic parents may escape some of the damaging effects if removed from their environment at an early age.

There is no cure for NPD, but symptoms can improve if treated properly. Treatments can make it easier to maintain relationships, feel close to others, and function independently.

Some research indicates that the first symptom of NPD is an exceptionally entitled attitude, which draws people in and leads them to believe they deserve more than they do. Young children are not yet able to make such distinctions; they are unable to recognize how much should be given to them and how much is their due. They may, for example, think that everyone deserves to be rich and popular. They may also believe that they should be treated better because they have a "special" personality.

The Narcissistic Spectrum Disorder

Many observers have noted the close relationship between narcissism and self-esteem. Self-esteem is often impaired in narcissists. In one study, 60% of a group of patients with NPD had significantly impaired self-esteem on a scale devised by psychoanalyst Heinz Kohut (1984). It seems that narcissists cannot give themselves credit for their achievements, so they are left with nothing but a grandiose façade. The lack of an inner source of self-esteem leaves narcissists feeling empty and lacking self-confidence. They need to be admired by others to feel adequate. The love and admiration of others can become a way of making up for the lack they feel inside. The positive feedback of adulation, receiving applause and awards, or other forms of attention may compensate narcissists because they respond intensely to these events. But people with NPD will never truly appreciate them because they lack self-worth.

A connection between narcissism and Borderline Personality Disorder has also been suggested. This connection has received support from a functional neurological perspective.

On the other hand, narcissism can be distinguished from Obsessive-compulsive Personality Disorder by the degree to which those with the former are concerned about high self-worth and perfection (rather than order, discipline, and rules). Narcissism may also be differentiated from psychopathy in that narcissists typically show more concern for social norms than psychopaths who don't think much about society as a whole.

Although narcissism may be related to psychopathy and Borderline Personality Disorder in some ways, it is typically less severe. However, narcissism can have features of both psychopathy and depression. There have been numerous reports of narcissistic behavior paired with depression in the media. However, in most cases, no formal association has been established between these two disorders.

Some traits of narcissism (such as passionate dedication to a cause or idea) are shared with other disorders.

Though it has been proposed that brain abnormalities and biology may cause certain narcissistic traits such as grandiosity, this hypothesis is unlikely to be true due to the range of participant groups involved in studies in this area. Studies examining the brains of NPD patients and non-NPD participants have not found evidence supporting this hypothesis. One study has found that excessive tolerance of narcissistic traits (rather than impaired self-evaluation) may be linked to hyperactivity in an area of the brain associated with emotion, impulse control, and decision making. This is seen in some people with NPD.

Narcissism may be linked to other traits and disorders, but the relation of narcissism to other conditions is complex. No studies indicate that narcissism is a cause of or a risk factor for substance abuse, bipolar disorder, antisocial personality disorder, or schizophrenia. On the other hand, research does indicate that narcissists are more vulnerable to feelings of stress and can be depressed when stressed.

CHAPTER 4: WHAT CAUSES NARCISSISTIC PERSONALITY DISORDER?

Many pathways can lead one to become a narcissist. The narcissistic pathway is not precise, direct, or even consistent. It is more of a maze with many forks along the way; it depends on what happens at each fork in the road. The outcome will depend on genetics, environment, and social interactions like peers and family members. There is no exact science to how one becomes a narcissist; it is more of a question of what happens at each fork in the road. The outcome will depend on genetics, environment, and social interactions like peers and family members.

The narcissistic pathway begins in the womb. There are important aspects to the development of narcissism:

Genes

Environment can affect the individual's response to certain genes, leading to a narcissistic personality. Some people are predisposed to narcissism, and others are vulnerable to narcissistic injury. The environment can also affect how one responds to gene stimulation, but that is not as significant as it may seem. The environment will determine whether someone is vulnerable or not. Still, overall many factors play a role in developing narcissism, including how someone receives stimulation from their family and peers. This can affect someone by playing off their environment and genetic predisposition.

Social Experiences

One's social experiences and the opportunities they provide determine how they develop socially: who they interact with, how they interact with them, where they sleep at night, what they eat for dinner, etc. For instance, a child with narcissistic parents is more likely to develop narcissism because of the parenting they experience. The child learns to expect praise, affection, and attention from their parents or other authority figures. The child does not have regular childhood friendships and instead is taught to focus on their own needs. This can ultimately affect the person's social skills and confidence, affecting how they react to situations later in life. If a person has few opportunities for socialization with peers, this can be a recipe for disaster. This can happen even if there are more than enough people to help them grow up and develop socially, but they choose to focus on themselves, which is a characteristic of narcissism. Some of the most common social experiences that contribute to narcissism are:

Peer Rejection

Children who receive peer rejection seem to grow into very sensitive adults and are more prone to becoming narcissists. This seems to be a common occurrence in narcissists. The social rejection can lead them to become self-centered, and they may seek out a narcissistic supply as a result.

It is common for peer-rejected children to have difficulty making friends later in life, contributing to their selfish behavior.

Peer Victimization

When children are victimized by their peers, they need to seek attention because otherwise their peers do not pay them any mind. This can cause the child to become an attention seeker, which is one of the characteristics of narcissism. This can be a result of social exclusion or having few friends.

Sibling Rivalry

Sibling rivalry can be a very influential factor in developing narcissism in children. A child who is shamed or rejected by their siblings may become a narcissist to gain attention from them. Siblings are often the first people that a child interacts with, and the relationship they form will determine how they interact with other people later in life. Children who grow up competing for parental attention and favoritism tend to develop narcissistic personality traits which can last into adulthood if nothing changes.

Being Spoiled by Parents

Children who are given everything they want without working for it learn to expect rewards without earning them. This sets them up for disappointment later because life does not always reward narcissists for their behavior. This expectation of being rewarded for nothing can come back to haunt them later in life and cause problems with careers and relationships, especially if they expect preferential treatment from others. This can happen while someone is still a child, and the parents are often oblivious to this happening. Parents who spoil their children set them up to become narcissists because it is not realistic or fair to expect or receive everything you want when you want it.

Childhood Exposure to Abuse

It is common for children who experience childhood abuse to become narcissists. Childhood abuse can cause emotional stress and damage them emotionally, mentally, and physically. This can harm the child's overall development, especially their ability to relate to others. This can result in them losing confidence and trust in others, becoming more narcissistic as an adult. This is often an issue when someone grows up with narcissistic parents or other abusive adults because they are often unaware of the abuse they have experienced until later in life.

Exposure to Alcohol or Drugs

A person exposed to alcohol or drugs at a young age can become a narcissist because of the way the drugs affect their brain development. Alcohol and drug abuse can harm a person's ability to develop normally. This can lead them to become socially awkward and increases the likelihood of them seeking attention from others due to low self-esteem.

Lack of Social Experiences

People who do not go out in public or have friends outside of their family do not develop socially, leading them to be more selfish as adults. This is especially true if they are not encouraged by the people around them daily. If someone does not have the opportunity to be around other people or practice proper social skills, it is unlikely they will develop them when they are out of their safe environment.

Parents with High Expectations

High expectations from parents can make it difficult for their children to grow socially. This can be due to the parents' own social issues. They could be trying to make up for their lack of social development, so they put pressure on their child to be what they never could be.

Self-disclosure

People who do not share personal information about themselves feel that they are not important. They do not see the value of sharing their inner thoughts and secrets with others because they think they are unimportant. If a person does not develop this aspect of socialization, they will likely become narcissistic or have narcissistic traits.

Social Support

People who do not get social support from their parents or family members have low self-esteem and become more narcissistic. Social support is one of the most significant factors for properly socializing in childhood, and if a child does not receive it, problems will arise later in life. People with low self-esteem often do not see the value in getting social support and neglect to develop the skills necessary to receive and give it. Those who do not receive this support may feel alone and isolated, leading them to focus on themselves more.

Family Instability

When families are unstable, children often try to please their parents with little success. This is often a reaction to being abused or neglected, especially if they are made fun of in front of others. They might handle this by becoming more narcissistic when they are older to gain attention from their family.

Sexual Abuse

If a person was abused sexually in childhood, they might react by becoming narcissistic. This is often a desperate attempt to gain attention and approval from others. Sexual abuse often causes emotional and mental damage that can cause lifelong problems, especially when not reported or disclosed to others. People who have been sexually abused often feel unworthy, and manipulation is a way for them to get what they want from others and feel better about themselves. When they are not given quality socialization skills, they become narcissistic as an adult because of the lack of support from their family or friends.

Media Intake

People who constantly consume entertainment media such as television, movies, and music are often more selfish. They do not see the negative aspects of the media, instead believe what they see in it is real life – or should be.

Sensory-processing Issues

When a person's sensory processing abilities are not working properly, they often have social problems. This can be due to learning disabilities or sensory processing issues resulting from brain damage from abuse or neglect during childhood. This manifests because the person cannot pick up on social cues that they are not receiving approval from others. As a result, they become more narcissistic because they need to prove themselves and make others like them.

Brain Damage

People born with brain damage may become narcissists as adults because their brains were changed. Brain damage can result from abuse or neglect during childhood. Those born with brain damage are also more likely to become narcissists because they do not socialize properly.

Antisocial Personality Disorder (APD)

People with APD often become narcissistic because they lack empathy. They do not feel emotions when they hurt others and recognize their pain. This can lead to them getting away with their actions and causing more harm in their lives because they are not being held accountable for their actions. If they become aware of their narcissistic tendencies, they can seek help to work on the underlying issues that caused the behavior.

Borderline Personality Disorder (BPD)

People with BPD often have a lot of love to give but do not properly show it. They may be seeking approval from others and trying desperately to win over their attention. The lack of quality socialization skills they developed during childhood causes them to react in ways that make it impossible to receive what they need. They become narcissistic because their self-esteem is low and their self-worth is high. They do not see the value in others, and they react to this by becoming narcissistic.

Anxiety Disorders

People with anxiety disorders often have social issues as children because they are constantly worried about performing well in front of others. The constant fear of failure can cause them to obsess over what other people are thinking, which leads them to focus on themselves and become more narcissistic. They may also have constant fears of abandonment and feel that if people leave them or hate them, they will be alone forever. Because anxiety is a symptom that something is wrong in a person's life, a therapist should diagnose it while they are still young so that they can receive proper treatment and recover more quickly.

What happens to your brain when a narcissist raises you?

Emotional, physical, and developmental problems can arise for children who narcissistic parents. There is a strong link between being raised by a narcissist and having an almost perpetual sense of hurt and confusion in adult life. This pain can lead to shame, anguish, and depression in adulthood as the child feels stuck in an unarticulated state of emotional neediness that no one else can provide.

Neediness

These children are needy as adults with abandonment issues they feel they must fill to numb their pain. This is because they have not learned how to bring their needs into the open or express them openly, so they must find other ways to deal with the emotional pain of being abandoned or rejected.

Intimacy Issues

These children are taught to avoid looking for love and connection because they have not learned how to care for others and give appropriately. They have a strong desire to connect with others and be cared for, so they spend most of their early years looking for the wrong person to provide care and alleviate their suffering. This leads many people with Narcissistic Personality Disorder into codependent relationships where they become fixated on someone who can provide a temporary sense of security.

A Sense of Being Unlovable and Misunderstood

These children feel an overarching sense of being unlovable and misunderstood because they have not learned how to love or understand themselves. They feel an overwhelming sense of pain, and they spend time trying to dodge the wounds their parents created in them. This can lead to drug abuse, alcoholism, depression, anxiety disorders, and eating disorders, as these people feel as though they cannot escape the pain of their past or how they were raised. They become narcissistic to cope with this trauma by focusing on themselves without ever working through the emotional wounds that led them down a dark path in life.

Brain Abnormalities in Narcissism

Narcissists have larger volumes of gray matter in their amygdalae than non-narcissists. People with Narcissistic Personality Disorder have more connections between the amygdala and the dorsolateral prefrontal cortex. This means that when a narcissist is experiencing a strong emotional response, it causes a stronger response that makes it difficult to calm down. Their amygdala is also triggered by things that other people would not react so strongly to or at all. This causes the person with a Narcissistic Personality Disorder to focus only on themselves because they are not receiving enough attention from others. They are constantly being threatened by something their parents said or did while they were growing up.

Low activity in the frontopolar cortex has been observed in people with Narcissistic Personality Disorder. This means that when they focus on a particular task and work with other people, they cannot shift their attention to something else when it becomes more important. Their brain cannot shut off the part of itself that is focused on themselves, so they become stuck in one-track thinking and never learn how to take a step back and look at everything from another perspective. This can cause them to assume other people are out to get them or try to convince them of something bad.

Rapid Switching Between Emotions

When narcissists feel good in one moment and bad in the next, they cannot develop their unique emotional response. The brain parts involved in emotional recognition become confused because the amygdala becomes triggered way too quickly. This causes them not to develop an understanding of how they feel. They may be positive one minute and then angry the next, or happy one minute and then sad the next without being able to explain why this is happening. They are more worried about how they feel than with the situation, and as a result, they are unable to put themselves in another's shoes when needed.

Lack of Moral Reasoning

Moral reasoning and pain empathy are reduced in narcissism. Narcissists have less of a capacity to associate with others on an emotional level when thinking about a moral dilemma. The cold and rational way they see situations causes little compassion for other people experiencing pain. This can cause them to become self-centered and only think about what will benefit them, instead of anyone else. This means they are more likely to take advantage of someone else when they are vulnerable and less likely to help someone else if they need it.

Difficulties in Decision Making

Decision making involves automatic processes related to emotional responses rather than logical analysis. People with Narcissistic Personality Disorder often cannot see their choices in the context of personal morality and cannot decide how they feel about situations or people. They may seem cold and unaffected by a situation, but this mask hides the fact that they have no moral compass or ability to make ethical decisions. As a result, they make terrible choices in relationships, business, and any other situation where a strong sense of right and wrong is required.

Reduced Behavioral Inhibition

Behavioral inhibition is reduced in people with Narcissistic Personality Disorder. They often become overwhelmed and unable to divert their attention away from themselves. This is because the amygdala tells them that they need to focus on what is important right now and they become lost in it without realizing the danger of not managing their thoughts and feelings. They are more likely to do things that will make them feel good at the moment without thinking about how it will affect themselves or others, but this can cause harm down the line.

How the Brain Reacts to Trauma

Brain scans of people with Narcissistic Personality Disorder show that those with this disorder significantly differ in the frontal cortex than those without it. The frontal lobes control an individual's executive functions, including self-regulation and problem-solving. Having these problems functioning can cause someone to act out in a number of ways that are not socially acceptable. The amygdala is activated when an individual experiences strong emotions like fear and anger, especially when coupled with certain situations or circumstances. Because people with NPD have smaller frontal cortexes, so they can no longer use logic to assess situations for "normal" behavior. When something bad happens and then triggers a strong reaction, the amygdala works with the hypothalamus by releasing cortisol into the brain. It causes their blood pressure to rise and redirects blood flow into their muscles to improve their chances of survival if they need to fight back or run away.

This can cause an individual to find themselves in a negative emotional state and unable to stop the damage they are causing. Then they will either act out their aggressive behavior or experience symptoms of post-traumatic stress disorder. Because their emotions are not healthy, it can also affect their ability to make good choices for themselves or others and maintain healthy relationships. They may have trouble thinking about any consequences from their actions or insensitive remarks.

How the Brain Reacts to Being Abandoned

People with this disorder have a high chance of experiencing abuse or neglect in their childhood. This may cause their brains to react in a damaging way when they become adults, and someone tries to leave them, especially if it is their first relationship. Their amygdala becomes activated and tells their hypothalamus to release cortisol so their body can prepare itself for harm. This can trigger symptoms of post-traumatic stress disorder.

The amygdala takes over the brain centers that control emotion and behavior, so it becomes difficult for someone with this disorder to reason about how they feel about what happened. They often struggle to control their emotions and recognize social boundaries. They may act out in an embarrassing way or make dramatic changes in how they act around other people. This behavior can make it hard for them to build new relationships. They may feel distant from anyone who tries to reach out to them, so they will have to learn how to reconnect with people if they want real relationships in their life.

Knowing how an individual's brain is wired differently can help us better understand why they behave so inappropriately. It can also help us think of ways to help them connect with others and release the pain that has been hidden away inside. We will then be able to react correctly by either reaching out and helping someone who needs it or moving on when they are not interested in receiving our aid.

CHAPTER 5: CORE TRAITS

People with different types of NPD often have the same traits, so they appear to be the same. But their behaviors and symptoms are different, which can make it harder to tell if they are having problems because of their personality or another issue. Suppose someone has many of the same characteristics as someone with narcissism but does not share other symptoms. In that case, it is important to check if there could be something else causing their behavior.

People with various types of NPD have 'core traits.' These include:

Lack of Empathy

This is a lack of sense of compassion or understanding of others and a lack of sympathy, pity, or tender feelings for someone else's pain and emotions. Individuals with this personality disorder are frequently indifferent to your distress. This trait might manifest in everyday life as hostility and irritability towards others. For example, they might be cold and mean to those around them, especially people they do not know. They do not care if you are unhappy, and they might have anger outbursts without any provocation.

Chronic Feelings of Emptiness or Boredom

A lack of empathy is often intertwined with chronic feelings of emptiness. People with this personality disorder often feel bored, empty, and lacking emotion. People who do not have this condition might experience despair when they feel empty, but those with narcissistic personality disorder are unaware. They can function normally, and they do not see their emptiness. When people have a life that mirrors their insides and contains little meaning, it is considered one reason why they become narcissistic in the first place. This can manifest in frantic attempts to be happy in everyday life, such as alcohol and drug abuse, risky behavior, and reckless driving. Another manifestation would be the desire for material possessions and an obsession with wealth.

Needing Constant Admiration

People with this personality disorder have a deep need for admiration. They have an inflated ego, a feeling of superiority over others, and a sense of entitlement. This is why they constantly feel as though they are better than others and seek to outshine them at everything they do, no matter how small the competition is. They crave compliments, attention, and praise. They want to feel needed and valued, and they often make themselves the center of attention. If they do not get the admiration they desire, or if others do not give them enough praise, people with this personality disorder become angry and blame the world for their failure. This can also make them lash out in anger at those around them, including their children.

The Drive to Win and Be the Best

People with Narcissistic Personality Disorder are often driven by an inner need to be number one and win at everything. Those with this condition constantly want to be better than anyone else, which is why they often set goals that are too high. They lack patience, and they do not like the feeling of being in second place. It makes them angry, so they might resort to cheating or sabotaging someone else's success to feel more satisfied. They often underestimate others, and will push people around in an attempt to get the respect and the reaction they want.

Exploitation

People with this condition like to use others for their own benefit. They like to manipulate and deceive others, but they often deny doing so. For example, a friend might invite them somewhere, but they will not show up because they do not feel like it at the last minute. They will then use excuses such as traffic or a change of plans. People with NPD exploit people in other ways as well. For example, they might borrow money and then ignore the other person's requests to pay it back. They might also take advantage of employees.

A Sense of Entitlement and Expecting Special Treatment

People with this condition have a sense of extreme entitlement. Others are expected to show them respect, give in to their demands, and cater to their wishes at all times. They believe that they are better than everyone else and above the rules. They will not tolerate anyone trying to tell them what to do or how to act because they believe they know everything. They think they should do whatever makes them happy, even if it hurts others or breaks the law. If they do not get the admiration, attention, or praise they expect, they might become angry. The person with this personality disorder might lash out at others or sabotage their relationships by spreading rumors or breaking trust.

Exhibitionism

Individuals who suffer from this condition have an overwhelming desire to flaunt themselves—often to the point of being vain and self-absorbed. They like to wear flashy clothing showing off their bodies, make a scene at parties where everyone can see them, and wear makeup covering up their imperfections. However, clothing and makeup do not fix anything or give them any real sense of comfort or confidence. People with this condition have no real opinions and only care about what others think of them. This can manifest in everyday life as being overly critical of others.

Grandiosity

People with this personality disorder often have an inflated sense of self-importance. They tend to value confidence and talent more highly than skills and accomplishments. They believe that their ideas are always correct, and that no one can ever compare to what they have to offer. They usually have an overbearing attitude, even though they may have no idea what they are talking about. People with NPD are usually unaware of their grandiose nature.

Difficulty Trusting Others

This condition makes it hard for people to trust others. They are not particularly good at giving compliments or respecting others for their achievements. They become angry at those who show admiration to other people instead of showing the same amount of respect to them.

Inappropriate Hostility and Anger

People with this condition find it difficult to be friendly or outwardly kind to others. They tend to choose friends who mirror their sense of self-importance, which makes them feel good about themselves. They will often enter into relationships where they only care about themselves and do not think much about their partner's feelings. This can be a lonely existence, but they may not realize it. People with NPD are often angry and hostile because they feel that they are the only people in the world who deserve respect, admiration, and praise.

Disregard for Right and Wrong

This condition makes it hard for people to distinguish between right and wrong. They enjoy blaming others for their mistakes and despise anyone who tells them no. They can become very angry when they do not get what they want or cannot get their way. This can manifest in extreme responses to minor incidents or stubbornness on the other person's part. They might start arguments without reason and react very strongly to anything not aligned with them. People with Narcissistic Personality Disorder frequently believe they are correct, even when they are not.

Inflated Sense of Self-Worth or Self-Esteem

People with this condition can have a distorted view of themselves. Even though others think otherwise, they think of themselves as worthy, good-looking, talented, and friendly. They do not recognize their flaws and often lie about who they are and what makes them special. People with this condition often show off to the world without realizing it or caring.

A Need for Stimulation

People with this condition want constant reassurance that they are fascinating and important. They need constant praise, attention, and adoration from others to feel worthy. They feel very anxious if they do not get these things from others. They also expect others to behave in ways that mimic how they feel about themselves, such as having one-sided conversations about themselves only. People with NPD do not like people who do not admire them or give them attention.

Shallow Emotions

People with this condition are often weak in expressing their feelings and emotions. They usually feel very lonely because they think no one understands them or wants to be around them. However, they cannot notice or care about anyone else's feelings. This can create issues in their lives, but they rarely think about changing their behavior. Most people with this disorder have trouble identifying and expressing emotions, so it can be hard for them to react appropriately in many situations. They might put up a tough exterior and try to persuade people that they care, but they often fail.

Taking Criticism Personally

People with this condition tend to think that they are superior to everyone else. This can cause many problems in their lives, but they usually do not notice it or care to change it. They choose friends who help them feel good about themselves, so those friends usually reinforce their beliefs about themselves. When people start criticizing or disagreeing with them, they feel like those people are attacking them on purpose and want to hurt or embarrass them in front of an audience.

Tendency to Blame Others for Their Feelings

People with this condition make it hard for themselves by blaming others for their feelings. They think that the world revolves around them and that anyone who fails to give them what they want is betraying them. This can cause many problems in their lives because it makes it hard for others to provide things that people with Narcissistic Personality Disorder truly need, like affection or love.

Impulsive Behaviors

People with this condition can get very angry when they do not get their way or if someone is trying to put them down. They might start arguments without provocation and break down emotionally in public just because someone mentioned something that angered them. People with this condition have no regard for their own safety, so they might even put themselves in danger, doing stupid things that could harm or kill them.

Disregard for the Safety of Others

People with this condition rarely feel the need to put others' interests before their own. They don't care if someone gets hurt in order to get what they want, and they'll even lie about who started an argument or did something wrong in order to get away with it. They feel like they are always right because no one else understands them as they do. They usually have a hard time apologizing and admitting that someone else could be right when they were wrong because it would mean that they were wrong and that someone knew better than them. It would also mean that they were not perfect on some level, which they always tend to believe.

Disregard for the Safety of Themselves

People with this condition might have a lot of self-confidence, but they often have no regard for their well-being. They are more concerned about how others perceive them. They might do dangerous things for no reason or hurt themselves in ways that can cause permanent injury just because someone upset them. When they argue with someone, they feel like fighting is an accomplishment, even if it can harm one or both of them.

Withdrawal from Relationships

People with this condition have no sense of when to stop talking about themselves and what they want. They do not know how to create bonds and close contact with others, so they often die alone. It is very important for them to feel special and admired by their friends, so if people start putting them down or disagreeing with them, they may get angry or upset. People with Narcissistic Personality Disorder are often lonely because they are oblivious to other people's distress and thus have no idea when to stop talking or apologize.

Self-Centeredness

People with this disorder always need to feel like the center of attention, so they may be very dramatic in their reactions to things that happen in their lives. If they cannot get the things they want, they may get angry or break down emotionally. However, they usually know how to play "sad" or "caring" to get what they want. Since most people with NPD are not very good at expressing themselves, those feelings might come out in what people perceive as a temper tantrum rather than an appropriate reaction to a disagreement or loss.

Inability to Remember Details

People with this condition often find it hard to keep details straight, especially names and dates. They tend to skip over important parts of conversations, and ignore other people's feelings. They focus on what they want to talk about and forget that they could be causing hurt feelings by not listening properly.

Low Self-Esteem

People with this condition might never feel good enough, smart enough, or pretty enough. They need a lot of attention and admiration from others to feel good about themselves, so they will find ways to get it.

Inability to Say No

People with this condition sometimes have a hard time saying "no" when someone wants them to do something for them. They might even agree to things they do not understand, or that would hurt them.

Making a Good First Impression

People with this condition are very good at making a good first impression. They know how to act to get anyone to like them. They might do whatever people want to make them happy and special, at the beginning of a relationship. However, their partner usually ends up feeling empty and unhappy when the narcissists true colors inevitably begin to show.

Unrealistic Perception of Romantic Relationships

People with this condition may not know how to evaluate romantic relationships because they do not allow anyone to get close to them. They might expect the person they love to always be there for them and put them above all of their other relationships. They may think that if their loved one does not always agree with what they want, the person does not care about them or is going through a personal problem. They will often change themselves or pretend to be someone who can fill in whatever void is missing in the other person's life.

People with this condition get angry or hurt if people do not have positive opinions of them. People with NPD usually do not understand that no one can make everyone happy all of the time, so they try harder to maintain their relationships and usually fail at it. They can be very lonely and insecure, but they do not know what is wrong. They need to learn to trust someone without expecting too much attention, approval, or affection. They need to learn to please others without trying to be someone they are not. They need to learn to be responsible, honest, and direct with people. People who suffer from this disorder are often unaware that they have a problem and refuse to seek help. If they are forced into counseling, they usually want to talk about themselves without listening to anyone else's feelings.

Life Stages of the Narcissist

There are several life stages of the narcissist, each with different symptoms. Early diagnosis and intervention can help the person grow emotionally.

The following are some important life stages:

Early Childhood (3-5 years)

The mental disorder's personality traits can be seen as early as three years old. The child is less social and demands attention frequently. They may act spoiled or superior to other children and adults. They may have problems with other students who have behavioral issues at school, or they may not get along with their parents or caregivers at home. The child may refuse to do their homework and complain about their teachers or siblings. They may also refuse to participate in group activities or be very competitive in school games. These behaviors could result from mental illness or just a bad attitude.

Pre-Teenage (10-14 Years)

The child's emotional problems become difficult to hide by this age. The child might have mixed emotions, such as not wanting others to know how they feel and wanting attention. They might have trouble forming friendships and make up rumors about people at school. They might be very sensitive to criticism and express anger or violence when told they are wrong. They usually blame their problems on someone else and exaggerate them.

Teenage (15-18 Years)

The child's symptoms often turn into serious emotional problems at this age. They might have problems with authority, family, friends, or school. The child might become violent or suicidal if they do not get what they want and blame others for everything wrong in their lives. They may think everyone is out to hurt them and that no one will ever like them for who they are. They are often very out of touch with their feelings, and they think they know the right way to do something. The child cannot understand the consequences of their actions or how their behavior will affect other people.

Early Adulthood (18-30 Years)

The adult has grown up and still has severe emotions. They may have a strong grip on others and will not listen to anyone who disagrees with them. They may have difficulty forming relationships and trusting another person. They might be very hostile and aggressive when dealing with others, or even family members they feel do not care about them or respect their authority. They will blame things that go wrong on other people and justify their actions while keeping control. They will usually avoid taking responsibility for anything in their lives.

Mature Adult (30+ Years)

The adult might still be very dependent on others. They might have many problems with authority and try to find ways to make them look bad in front of others. They have a hard time understanding how their actions affect others and may act like a child if they do not get what they want. At this stage, the person might be living an independent life, but they continue to have damaging emotions and struggle to trust others. They are still very emotional and might be jealous, angry, fearful, or sad. They might have relationships with people who care about them but are afraid to let anyone in on their true feelings.

All forms of NPD can be treated. If the treatment is successful in the long run, the person will be less dependent on attention from others.

The following are common treatment strategies used by psychiatrists:

Psychotherapy

The therapist will help the person understand their emotions and deal with them in a healthy manner that does not worsen the symptoms or cause more suffering. The therapist will help the person learn about themselves, their emotions and deal with people healthily.

Psychoanalysis

The therapist will ask the person many questions about their life and figure out why they have certain emotions and behaviors. The therapist will try to get to the core of what is causing the problem by dealing with their emotions and removing some of the external factors causing them to act the way they do. They also try to help the person understand why they have certain behaviors and how they affect their relationships and mental stability.

Family Therapy

This kind of therapy helps address unresolved problems between family members. The therapist will teach parents how to handle their child and prevent their damaging behavior. Parents usually have a hard time dealing with a child who has NPD because it can cause stress in the parent-child relationship and make them feel like they cannot trust each other. The therapist will help the parents understand why their child acts the way they do and how to deal with it.

Biofeedback

Biofeedback is a popular treatment method that uses sensors on the patient's head and face to monitor muscle tension and relaxation. The patient wears eye goggles connected to a computer screen, and the muscles in their face are shown in moving colors on the screen. When they tense up, the colors change to red, and when they relax, it will turn into blue or yellow. The patient must relax their face muscles entirely to make the colors go green. The goal is for the patient to learn how to control their facial muscles and fight off NPD symptoms. Biofeedback may also show that their body will react negatively when they get agitated or angry, so they can learn how to control it and fight it off by relaxing.

Narcissistic Personality Disorder is often confused with Borderline Personality Disorder, which has several common characteristics with NPD. Still, instead of being fearful of abandonment or people hurting them, NPD sufferers are afraid that others might leave them or that no one will ever like them (fear of rejection) if they face their real emotions.

Medications can be used to treat Borderline Personality Disorder, but they cannot be used to treat NPD.

Fortunately, many people who have NPD can go through life without their condition negatively affecting them. They might still have problems in their relationships and have some angry outbursts from time to time, but they will not cause major harm to themselves or others. They may, however need assistance from professionals in order to do so. The family of a person with NPD may get frustrated since they cannot control the behavior and might think the best thing to do is let the person go through life alone. However, will not help them stop hurting themselves or others, and it will not solve their problems.

CHAPTER 6: COMMON SIGNS THAT YOU HAVE A NARCISSISTIC MOTHER

It is sometimes difficult to recognize that someone close to us has a narcissistic personality. Narcissistic Personality Disorder is a mental health condition that causes a person to have an inflated sense of self-importance. Narcissists will do anything to ensure they are the center of attention, even if it means using those close to them as an audience, leading to painful relationships. The effects of having this type of mother are often particularly obvious in the children she brings into the world.

The following are several of the most common indicators that your mother is a narcissist:

Her Love is Conditional

If a mother gives her children conditional love, this will leave scars on their psyche and make them feel lost or unworthy. This type of mother's love will be restricted to certain behaviors and depends on children performing sufficiently or "keeping up appearances." A narcissistic mother makes her children believe that they are not important enough for unconditional love and that only certain types of behavior will get a reward. They learn to doubt themselves, thinking that something must be wrong because they don't feel loved unconditionally, and they don't know why not. An adult child of a narcissistic mother can set out to earn that love through highly specific and often unnecessary behaviors.

A narcissistically inclined mother also sometimes relates to her young-adult children on a case-by-case basis. She becomes upset when they can't measure up to adult standards and fails to show them any empathy or understanding that they are still learning and growing into their adult selves. This cannot be very clear for the child if the mother treats him as an adult in one situation and then expects him to act like a child in another situation. It's confusing for children to meet adult standards of behavior before they understand what those standards mean, which reinforces their sense of not being good enough.

Co-dependency

If a narcissistic mother treats her children like her cats or dogs, this is also likely to impact them negatively. She will often treat them like babies who need constant care and attention. It's common for children who have been raised by a narcissistic mother to feel that no one else will take care of them, especially when they grow up and realize that their only relationship was with their mother. Narcissistically inclined mothers are often demanding and opinionated mothers who tell little lies, hinting at hidden agendas. These mothers use guilt and blame or put children down to make them feel they must do everything she asks. Children who have grown up in this way often feel like they are still under their mother's control because she will constantly remind them of their inability to come through on any responsibility that's asked of them. They often feel like they cannot make decisions for themselves, and that there is no point in trying.

Setting Unrealistic Standards

If a narcissistic mother sets high and unrealistic standards for her children, this can also leave a lasting impression on them. They will find these standards hard to measure up to and can often feel frustrated that they are not living up to them. The narcissistic mother usually expects her children to be the perfect example of what she wants them to be. She expects them to serve as role models for all of their friends and family. These mothers expect perfection in their offspring, meaning that no matter how hard they try, they will never measure up to these standards. They forget that these ideals are unrealistic and do not apply everywhere, especially not at home, where the most important thing is to have a good relationship with those in your life.

Being Overly Critical and Vindictive

If a narcissistic mother gets angry at her children, she can be harsh and unforgiving. She is not the type of mother who can easily laugh at mistakes or feel compassion for her children. She is not the kind of mother who can accept that her children have a mind of their own and can make mistakes. A narcissistic mother will sometimes show no empathy or sympathy for her child and will likely feel they deserve some form of punishment.

Narcissistic mothers sometimes take offense at things where there should be none, but their anger may serve as an unhealthy motivation for change. When she feels hurt, she will treat her children harshly to get them back for any perceived wrongs. She blames them for everything, does not respect their feelings, and does not empathize with them when they experience a personal loss. She will deflect her feelings onto her children and lash out at them with her anger. This makes children feel they can't discuss their feelings with their mother.

Neglecting Children's Needs and Emotional Security

Children of a narcissistic mother are often neglected in that the parents do not put their needs first. The narcissistic mother is not always physically or emotionally present for her children when they need her, and she does not consider how her actions will affect them on a deep level. The narcissistic mother often puts herself first in the family and the children before her husband, yet she expects them to be there whenever she needs something. She sees that her own needs are settled before considering anyone else's. She might also neglect the emotional security of her children by only paying attention to them when they please or impress her. She doesn't understand the inner psychological needs children have and only gives them attention when they are successful. Their self-esteem can suffer if they don't live up to their mother's standards, and yet she is always putting them down in her subtle way. Her children will feel insecure because they feel judged by someone who supposedly loves them yet seems so critical at the same time. Discipline is often excessive and never given to help a child learn from their mistakes, but rather to make them feel bad about themselves. They might also feel guilty or worthless for any perceived wrongs they have experienced at her hands.

Unable to be Introspective

A narcissistic mother will rarely ask herself questions or consider any of the things inside her. She seldom thinks about her own personal development, how she came to be the way she is, or what it is like to be in someone else's shoes. Children raised in this environment may have no idea who their mother really is and see her as a loving but controlling figure who can force them to do whatever she wants.

Suppressing the Child's Need for Attention

A narcissistic mother often doesn't give her children the attention they need because she is focused on what she wants instead. Her children can feel neglected when she does not give them the time or emotional support they desire. Children of this type of mother are often sexually abused by their family members. They are repressed when they reach adulthood because all of their care and affection was given to someone who could not care less about their needs and wants. They learn through tough times that no one loves them and can't rely on anyone else when they are rejected, neglected, or mistreated. As adults, they will often use sex as a tool to get what they want because it is the only way they can feel special or important to someone else. They look for a partner who they hope can fulfill them, yet they will subconsciously choose someone who will reject them too.

Dominant Lifestyle

A narcissistic mother has a dominant lifestyle where she is in total control of her family. She sees everything that is going on within her family and is highly critical of anyone who does not live up to her standards or expectations. A narcissistic mother often turns the child into an adult before they are ready to be so, which prevents them from being innocent and carefree. She makes her children be responsible for their lives and make decisions that they are not ready to make. They get so used to this way of life that they may not know any different.

Lack of Emotional Connection

Children of narcissistic mothers often feel alone with no one there for them when they are very young. They experience emptiness, loneliness, and despair. There is no connection with anyone, which keeps them from attaining valuable human connections later in life. Children of this type of mother often feel as though they were born to serve their family, and they struggle with holding on to their feelings and independence. They will have trouble trusting anyone because there is always something that can be taken from them, especially emotionally. This type of mother does not understand what love for another person is about. She feels isolated from everybody else's emotions and her own, making it very difficult for her children to know how they should feel and why.

Not Modeling the Best Behaviors for Her Children

A narcissistic mother often cannot control her own emotions but instead uses them to control her children. She will often use emotionally abusive punishments to break her children down, leading to low self-esteem and guilt for things they didn't do.

The topic of power is a crucial one with a narcissistic mother, and she uses it to draw a line between herself and everyone else around her. Children who grow up in this environment have very few role models to look up to because their narcissistic mother does not care about personal development.

A narcissistic mother can be selfish, unkind, hostile, and critical. This can affect her children in a variety of ways. They grow up feeling alone, unloved and confused about who they are. They may never learn how to love and be loved because they did not receive the best examples. They grow up feeling ashamed of who they are and what they want, so they may constantly seek acceptance from their mother by making her happy. This develops into a cycle where the child tries to please their narcissistic mother by doing much more than a normal child would, and they suffer needlessly due to their failure at accepting themselves.

CHAPTER 7: FATHERS' BEHAVIORS

In families with a narcissistic mother, fathers are often either absent or enable the mother's behavior. They, too, are victims of the mother's narcissism (and codependency), but they may not know it. Children who grow up in disordered families, such as with a narcissistic or borderline mother and an enabling father, are denied the opportunity to develop their full potential because they are caught in a cycle of chronic stress; they don't know how to cope with it, and it overwhelms them. Kids who grow up in such families develop a pattern of becoming incapacitated as a result of stress, thus perpetuating the cycle.

An enabling father often portrays himself as the all-wise, all-understanding father. He may have a great sense of humor and can make everybody laugh. He is the father who takes care of all the family's problems, worries, and concerns. Yet, he does not see his contributions to the problems. Typical codependent behavior on his part is to avoid conflict or criticism by giving in to his wife or doing what she wants. When he does this consistently for a long period, it becomes his personality. The children learn to have their reality constantly shaped and distorted by their mother and father—and later by their spouses—and so they grow up feeling they are living in a world that is not real. It is a never-ending, stressful situation where there are very thin lines between reality and their parents' distorted version of reality. As adults, these children are still frustrated by their inability to change their circumstances and achieve the success they desire. They are being driven by the same forces that controlled them in their family of origin. Children of narcissistic mothers may experience anger and sadness when their father is unable—or unwilling—to assist them in achieving their goals. They are frustrated and angry when they watch their mother get what they want while they're standing in line waiting to be served. Many adult children have learned that anger doesn't work, and it is safer to sit in silence until the moment is right for them to shout. So instead of being proactive, these children become re-active, leading to anxiety and depression because they are living out of control. Some adult children learn that the best way to get what they want from their partner is by being passive and not having a strong, assertive presence in the relationship dynam-ic. They don't want to be too demanding and pushy because they fear their partner will react negatively, so they sit and take whatever they are given. This serves their narcissistic needs even though it is the most dysfunctional way of communicating and handling problems.

In families with a narcissistic mother, the children are often blamed for their parents' problems. The children feel that if only things had been different in their family of origin, their life would have been much better. Children from such families often grow up feeling defective. They don't receive any validation from their parents and may not validate themselves. Because they are always defending themselves, they do not learn to trust their instincts and feelings. Many don't even know what is real because reality is so distorted in the home. Their emotions have become distorted and they are under the impression that everyone is out to get them.

Gripped by their parents' distorted view of reality and feeling they can never win, they learn to be passive, which is a very defensive way to be. It allows them to constantly challenge others and expect a reaction that justifies their anger, but few people will react in the same way over the same thing all the time. They will try any means necessary to control others because they feel that if they don't, they won't feel secure or safe.

Fathers who enable the mother's behavior play a central role in developing this problem. Though they know that the mother's behavior is unhealthy, they don't want to rock the boat by identifying and dealing with it. They have learned that expressing anger, disapproval, or criticism will lead to problems and it will be used against them. To avoid further conflict and the guilt they feel for not being able to help the children, they instead tolerate the mother's behavior in an attempt to keep the peace.

A father's ability to be emotionally available and nurturing is crucial for healthy child development. If a father enables a narcissistic mother, he will likely lack empathy and understanding for his children. He has learned not to be honest or reflective, so he cannot see the validity of his children's needs. As a result, he is often unable to help them when they're faced with difficult choices, sees the world in a distorted way, and feels uncomfortable with who they are and what they have become.

The children will feel the frustration of their circumstances and the guilt that they have failed to help themselves. Still, they don't know how to resolve their feelings because they can't trust—or even identify—themselves or anyone else. They are used to everything being wrong and everyone being unfair, so they have no way of knowing whether their feelings reflect reality. Their anger is misdirected toward everyone else to control the uncontrollable and regain a sense of power. This is usually done by passive-aggressive means like giving silent treatment or making sarcastic comments so that no one will notice the real problem. They want to feel powerful, but the only way they can achieve this is by being aggressive.

Adult children of narcissistic parents often feel that they are not as good as their siblings. They may believe that they were born at the wrong time or to the wrong parents because that would explain why things went so wrong for them. It may sound crazy, but this is very common for children of narcissistic mothers.

CHAPTER 8: AT FIRST GLANCE, A SEEMINGLY TYPICAL FAMILY

The rest of the world is unlikely to notice the link between your problems and your mother's actions. It may not be easy to see this link yourself because you were in a unique situation and may feel that you over-reacted. But you need to remember that that is what happened.

The rest of the world needs to understand what narcissism is and what it does, especially to the children of mothers with this condition. This can be a problem for several reasons:

They are not recognized as a problem by the authorities.

The authorities are often unaware of the serious personality disorder involved. They only see the narcissistic parent being difficult to deal with in some ways. The authorities can't speak up for you and offer protection from the narcissist because they don't understand what is going on. They are often afraid of unusual personalities and will back away from them.

Children do not receive any help from official sources.

It might take years for a judge – if one was ever appointed – to rule on a petition for custody. Children's services may help. You will have to describe the situation so that they see that it is abusive and that you deserve protection.

No one will take away a mother's right to her children if she is not doing anything harmful physically to them, even though they are being abused in another way. For example, if she hates discipline and won't let her chil-dren have rules or boundaries, no one will step in to enforce them.

People think you are the one acting strangely.

They may assume that you're unbalanced, lonely, and envious of your mother. They may assume that it's all your imagination. They may assume the worst about you and not be helpful at all. If your family gets involved at all, it may only be to support your mother's position or take their turn treating you badly as well.

People may not believe you are a victim

As children, we can feel powerless against our parents' abil-ity to ignore us and treat us harshly. As adults, we may feel powerless against their criticism of our treatment of them and our personality. This makes it difficult for those who have not been through this to understand the psychology involved or the extent of the abuse. Even if you explain it, they may not believe you. If you describe what happened to you, they may think you are unbalanced.

It will take a lot of patient explanation of your position and the facts to get your point across. You have to be very careful in how you present the facts to them. The sheer depth of lies, false fronts and betrayed emotions will have to be explained patiently to anyone who does not appreciate how a narcissist operates. They have to see the whole picture before they can be convinced of your sanity and, as a result, that she is abusive.

People may think you imagined the problem.

If people do not understand the true nature of your family's problems, they may assume that you have imagined the problem. They might think you are acting out of simple jealousy. It would assist if you could show them that you don't have any enemies other than your mother. If your family tends to avoid conflict, they may not want to get involved in something that looks like a personal dispute.

They don't want to accept her as the enemy.

They may not see her as an abuser. They think that you exaggerate what she's done to you or that you made it all up. Or, they might be fully aware of what she is doing to you but choose not to take your side. They don't want conflict, and they don't have the skills to deal with your mother if they try.

They may be afraid of losing their family status or position with her if they confront her about anything, even something as major as abusing her children. If she has been controlling, abusive, manipulative, and cruel for years, they have become used to living in fear of her wrath. They may believe that the status quo is the best. This could cause them to deny what they see.

They may not want to get involved in anything that looks like a personal dispute.

Similarly, if your family is well off financially or influential, they may concern themselves with keeping up the status quo. They might also fear losing their popularity by standing up to a narcissist. If they belong to a social group or club with her, they may want to avoid her wrath and other members' negative reactions. They may want to keep the peace at all costs, even if it means staying out of it.

You have likely been so affected by your experience that it is easy for peo-ple to believe you are emotionally disturbed. You will probably have difficulty expressing how you feel and why some things upset you more than others should. However, if no one in your family has ever heard of narcissism, they won't know what they are dealing with.

You have to show them facts. You can't expect people to change their opinions about you if they don't understand the extent of what your mother is doing to you. Explain how it feels when your mother tells you what she will do if you misbehave.

It is easy for them to disbelieve you when they cannot see how much damage she is doing. The messages they receive from their peers, family, and social groups can be more influential than the facts you are bringing to them. They will be extremely hesitant about making any changes to the family structure.

You don't have to explain everything about being abused by your mother to everyone in your family, but it is important to find support wherever possible.

CHAPTER 9: ADULT CHILDREN RAISED BY NARCISSISTIC MOTHERS: COMMON TRAITS

If you grew up with a narcissist for a mother, then you may have some difficulty owning your power and taking good care of yourself. Because the narcissist sets the example for how it is acceptable to be treated, a child can grow up without a strong sense of being loved or valued.

To have any hope of healing from narcissistic mother, these children need to learn how not only to love themselves but release their expectation of being taken care of by others. They need time and patience to establish boundaries that they would never have been allowed to have as children.

The following are traits that are common in adult children of narcissistic mothers:

Highly Self-critical

Narcissists are often intensely critical of their children, so when these children are adults, they may also be very critical of themselves and find it difficult to accept that they sometimes do things well.

Lacking Confidence and Difficulty Being Assertive

Children who narcissists raised often are shy and have trouble standing up for themselves. They grow up feeling invisible, so it is hard for them to be assertive when they need to set a boundary or say "no." Consequently, they tend not to ask for what they want or need. That can be a real problem when you are an adult and do not feel that you can ask your partner for help because you could never ask your mother for help.

Difficulty Expressing Emotions

As children, we are taught how and what to express by watching our parents. Narcissists do not always teach their children how to express anger, frustration, or pain, which means that they may have trouble feeling the full range of emotions. This can set them up for future abusive relationships.

Prone to Depression

If you are an adult child of a narcissist, you often have difficult relationships with other people in your life. You may feel
isolated from others and even have periods of feeling very sad
and depressed. Part of the reason is that you have trouble being
assertive or asking for what you need. You may also feel overwhelmed and filled with anxiety when it is time to express anger
or frustration.

Prone to Addictions

If you are an adult child of a narcissist, you may have trouble
accepting that it is okay to be assertive and get what you want.
Because of your difficulty with emotional expression, your only
option for expressing yourself is often doing things that are not
good for you. You may turn to drugs, alcohol, or overspend to
release your anger or frustration.

Having an Eating Disorder

You may have learned as a child that if you were invisible, then
no one would notice what you do or make demands on you.
Low self-esteem and, eventually, an eating disorder can result
from this. This can happen through starvation, binging, and
purging.

Fear of Abandonment

If you are an adult child of a narcissist, you often have difficulty believing that you are worthy of being loved or cared for. You may find it hard to trust other people because if no one ever cared for you as a child, why would they now? Adults who grew up with narcissistic mothers are often very afraid of abandonment. They may not trust other people because they do not trust their judgment or memory, and they fear making mistakes.

Problems with Forgiveness

Adults who grow up in environments where love was hard to come by or insecurity and fear were common may have trouble forgiving others, both for their good and for the good of others. They may find it hard to let go of their anger or frustration or the mistakes and hurts of others, even when they have done nothing wrong.

Difficulty Establishing Boundaries

You might have been raised with a very weak boundary between you and your mother. It can be very hard for you to say "no" to someone. As an adult, this makes it difficult for you to trust others or maintain healthy relationships.

Difficulty Asserting Your Needs

As a child, you may have had trouble expressing your true needs and wants. Your mother may have been very critical of you, so it was hard for you to own your thoughts, feelings, or wants. You might avoid doing so as an adult because you are afraid of upsetting others and being criticized. That can make it difficult to ask for what you need and want from others.

Difficulty Making Decisions

Children who grow up in families where others make all the decisions for them find it hard to make their own decisions as adults. They might be plagued by indecisiveness and trouble with even the smallest decisions in their lives.

Difficulty Maintaining Positive Relationships

Adults raised by narcissists often know that they need a circle of good friends and confidants. They may have trouble being alone with themselves and having a true friend or confidant whom they can trust to be there for them, and who will advise them in times of crisis.

Loss of Security

Adults who grow up with a narcissistic mother may have difficulty trusting others. That makes it hard for them to see themselves as worthy of other people's love or security. They may struggle to form a partnership because they do not know how to ask for what they require in their relationships or value their own needs.

Fear of False Relationships

You might have been raised by a narcissist who seemed to be very caring and nurturing for the first several years of your life. As a child, you might have even thought that she was the most wonderful mother in the world. It is not until later that you realize that behind that façade was a very mean-spirited, controlling person who was only interested in her own needs and desires. As an adult, it is hard for you to see if people are sincere or dishonest because you expect them to be just like your mother was. This can make it hard to trust others and form healthy relationships later in life.

Difficulty Giving Gifts

Adults who grow up with a narcissistic mother often find it hard to give someone else a gift. They may not know how to value someone else, so it is hard to give something from the heart. They might also be afraid of being judged if they give someone the "wrong" gift, which makes it difficult for them to be generous.

Difficulty Accepting Support

You may find it hard to accept help from others. As a child, your narcissistic mother might have taken all the care and attention that should have been yours, so you did not learn that it was okay to ask for help and support. As an adult, that is not easy to rectify.

A Fatalistic View of Life

You may have been raised in a very fatalistic way, under the impression that there were things that you could not control. That means that even though you know things about your life are out of your direct control, you do not try to act on those things which you can influence. You might think, for instance, "there is nothing I can do about this," which makes it hard for you to try to change something or yourself.

Seeing Others as a Source of Validation

Adults who grow up with narcissistic mothers often use other people to judge their worth. You may not know how to figure out whether or not you are good enough. You might be afraid that if someone sees your true self, they will not like or love you, making it hard to get close to other people. It is hard to see your good qualities when you are held up to the mirror of others' opinions.

A Need for Control

All children need healthy boundaries and security. However, when a narcissistic mother raises a child, she often does not have these things because she does not truly care about her child's needs and desires. She may make all of the decisions for her child and then try to control them. A child raised by this type of parent often feels like a prisoner in their own home, unable to trust that they will be safe or secure if they go outside their own home. That means that you might have a very strong need for control as an adult. You might feel like you do not want to be open with others because bad things may happen to you if you are not in control.

Viewing the World as Dangerous

You may have grown up with a very negative view of the world because of your mother's narcissism. You might not know how to trust others or be in a healthy relationship because you were raised by someone who was not a good example of love and generosity. You might also feel like other people are only out for themselves, so it is better to keep your guard up than to let people know where you are vulnerable.

Difficulty Understanding Emotions

Narcissists often do not use genuine emotions when speaking or reacting to others. They may even tell their children that they are too sensitive or imagining something when someone hurts them. That makes it hard for a child to connect with their own emotions and understand the emotions of others.

When you grow up with a narcissistic mother, you may have difficulty trusting what you feel in your heart. You might be afraid of expressing empathy or of saying no when other people want something from you that is good for them at your expense. You might also live under the illusion that other people only care about themselves, so they can never be there for you. That can make it hard to understand your own needs and wants as an adult because your relationship with yourself has been stunted by this kind of treatment from others.

Fear of Being Pushed Out

A narcissistic mother might have threatened to send you away if you did not comply with her rules, expectations, and demands. You might also have been told that you were "bad" or "irresponsible" when you misbehaved as a child. That can make it hard for you to believe that someone else would welcome your presence in their lives. As an adult, that fear of being rejected or punished by others can make it hard to be open and honest with friends or loved ones. You might also be afraid that they will leave you if they realize how weak or needy you are, making it difficult for them to connect with someone so emotionally insecure.

Fear of Rejection

A narcissistic mother might have rejected you or punished you when you failed to live up to her impossible standards. As a result, you might be afraid that other people will do the same thing.

As an adult, this fear can make it difficult for you to connect with others, particularly someone who might be able to help you heal and deal with your past. You might fear that if you give yourself to someone, they will leave you for someone more deserving. You might also fear that if you let someone know about your fears, they will not be there for you when you need them the most.

CHAPTER 10: IMPACT ON SELF-ESTEEM

Narcissistic mothers are not just selfish or self-obsessed individuals. They have a way of making everyone around them feel like they are not good enough. They try to put down everyone they meet, especially their children. A narcissistic mother might have said things to her kids that made them question who they are and what they did wrong. That can make it very difficult for that child to develop a positive relationship with themselves as an adult.

You may have been raised by a narcissistic mother who told you that you could never be good enough for her because something was missing in your personality. Or maybe she told you that your appearance was not good enough for her, and she found flaws in everything about how you looked. Maybe she just ignored you when people complimented you on something you did well.

These things might have made it feel like something was wrong with you. It was as if your mother took everything about your personality and turned it into a negative thing that would become a source of shame for the rest of your life. You might have questioned if there was anything about yourself that would not make someone else look down on you or reject you at every turn. When that happens, people often enter adulthood wondering why they do not have a good relationship with anyone around them. In contrast, they look to others to validate their worth and make them feel better about themselves.

When narcissistic mother raises children, they develop a low sense of self-worth and self-confidence. The problem is that the mother may be projecting how she feels about herself onto her children. She might be projecting feelings of shame or unworthiness onto them because she does not want to face her problems. As a result, you end up taking on those bad feelings about yourself, and you do not know how to let them go or change your perspective about yourself. You often feel like you have to walk on eggshells around other people so they do not reject you for who you are. It is difficult for people to have self-confidence when living with that fear.

You might have come to believe in your adulthood that there is something wrong with you and that you are not good enough. Or, you may feel like your accomplishments do not mean anything because nobody ever told you they were happy for you or proud of what you did. It may be hard for some people to attract healthy relationships into their lives even though they try very hard to do so. They may stay in abusive relationships because it hurts less than being alone. When you have low self-esteem and low self-confidence, it isn't easy to trust that someone will love you for who you are.

Some people feel like they are not worthy of being loved because their mother never accepted them for who they were. They do not feel worthy of a relationship because they were raised by a narcissistic mother and never received enough praise or approval. A person with these feelings about themselves may begin to look at the narcissist's flaws as defining their own identity. It is a way to justify why people treat them poorly. It is a bit like being told to take the blame for something that someone else did to you.

These feelings can take hold of people later in life. Many young adults end up having low self-esteem and low self-confidence, and they have not quite figured out what to do about it. They may wonder if they are unlovable because their mother never told them otherwise.

Hiding Pain and Suffering

The adult often ends up suffering in silence. They try to deal with the pain from childhood by being very hard on themselves or lashing out at other people. It is not easy for those raised by narcissistic mothers to understand what happened to them. The pain of not being accepted for who they are can lead to much anger later in life. They may direct their anger at those who reject them or at those who are somehow different from others. Narcissistic mothers often teach their children hatred toward certain types of people, whether they are based on social status, race, gender, or sexual orientation.

There is also a tendency to feel like you do not deserve love in any form. When that happens, you start to push people away because you do not want anyone to try and love you. You have been hurt too many times in the past to believe that love is real and something worth having in your life. In this sense, the narcissistic mother can prevent her child from having a healthy relationship with both themselves and others as an adult. The adult raised by a narcissistic mother will carry their pain with them and not let anyone get too close. They may even push people away and hurt others to hide their feelings. Narcissistic mothers teach their children how to be cruel, which is a way of coping with their pain and suffering.

People-pleasing to Feel Worthwhile and Valuable

People-pleasing might be the ultimate goal for people with narcissistic mothers. These mothers often tell their children that they need to please everyone and everything in the world to make them feel worthwhile. People-pleasing can lead to problems in relationships later in life. People-pleasing is often a way of getting approval from others, at the expense of your own wants and needs.

The adult with this personality shows very few outward signs of coping with their pain and suffering. They have not truly gotten over the pain from childhood and have not learned how to deal with it in healthy ways. Instead, they avoid confronting their feelings and emotions by pushing people away or trying to act happy all the time. They do not let anyone get close because they can never be sure if it will cause them to lose what little security they have in life. This can be a very lonely way to live.

Narcissistic mothers will often teach their children to be manipulative to get their way or avoid something that makes them uncomfortable. This can come across as abusive to other people and can make it very hard to have a healthy relationship with others.

The most important thing is to talk about your childhood, why you feel the way you do, and what happened. When you do this, you'll also understand yourself better and be able to try new ways of coping with your pain. Support groups help people deal with childhood issues or understand abuse in relationships. It is very important to get support from people who understand what you've been through and can help you manage your feelings.

CHAPTER 11: SONS AND DAUGHTERS - DIFFERENCES

Being raised by a narcissistic parent is a gendered experience. It makes a difference if your narcissistic parent was a mother or a father. And it makes a difference if you were a boy or a girl.

Of course, gender is not the only factor influencing a child's experience with a narcissistic parent. Additional factors include the number of children in the family, the parental dynamics, your base personality, the type of narcissist your parent was, and the number of narcissistic traits they displayed—however, gender matters.

Whatever gender you are, if your mother is a narcissist, you are likely to have many of the same experiences, including being a source of narcissism for your mother. Children are often relied upon by narcissists to make them feel good about themselves, superior to others, and to assist them in carrying out their plans to achieve their goals. Children of both sexes are a source of supply for narcissists and may be used to assist the mother in gaining power and superiority over the other parent or one of her children. While it may feel good to be a part of a winning team at the time, it can taint your perception of others and increase your risk of developing narcissistic tendencies yourself.

Narcissistic mothers frequently rely on secrets, lies, and gaslighting to maintain their position. Growing up in this environment can result in pressure, stress, and a distorted view of how the world works. Almost every child of a narcissistic mother suffers somehow, even if it is not immediately obvious. You may have suffered emotionally and psychologically, or perhaps you have been picked on, bullied, and abandoned by your family.

Sons of Narcissists

All narcissists' children suffer. However, sons of narcissistic mothers specifically experience diminished autonomy, self-esteem, and difficulties in future relationships, especially with women.

As we know, narcissism varies in severity and type and according to an individual's personality and values. Some narcissistic mothers are disinterested in their children, while others are excessively involved. Certain individuals exhibit an aggressive demeanor, while others exhibit a caring or seductive demeanor.

Although your experience may vary, the following are some common patterns that sons of narcissists may experience:

Neglect

Narcissistic mothers burdened by motherhood neglect their children while simultaneously berating and criticizing them—at times for being too needy or childlike. They require assistance themselves and are unable to meet their child's needs. They may demand that their young son "be a man," or they may manifestly favor one child while ignoring or belittling another. They induce guilt in their children and cause them to second-guess their choices and behaviors.

Optimism and Criticism

Numerous narcissistic mothers romanticize their infant son. They instill him with confidence and a sense of significance. As he matures and asserts his independence, she disparages his emerging individuality and attempts to correct and change him. She may brag about her son to her friends to bolster her ego but is critical of him at home. In response, he may rebel and incite her wrath, or he may attempt to appease her to gain acceptance. His fall from grace can be perplexing and distressing. It becomes even worse if another child is born. He forfeits his uniqueness, and sibling rivalry can be ferocious.

She overvalues her son while undervaluing his siblings and belittles them in public. The son is usually the favorite and assumes the role of "golden child," which can be gratifying and disappointing. If a daughter is the focus of attention, she may develop into a trophy child who compensates for the narcissist's shortcomings. Unsurprisingly, the narcissistic mother has difficulty accepting her children as separate individuals. She demands adoration and competes for their attention. Because she has no boundaries or limits, there will likely be clashes and conflicts over when to stop helping or cooperating with her demands—loyalty can become an issue and can lead to an inevitable break between family members. The son may feel burdened by the expectations thrust upon him and envy his siblings for not carrying the same burden.

Narcissistic mothers often resent their children, particularly their sons. As a result, they try to overpower them. They are more likely to put their adult sons down, ignore them, or belittle them than support and encourage their autonomy. They want control over their son's actions and what he feels or thinks. They may keep their sons close while his siblings move away—his dependence on her helps sustain her exaggerated sense of importance and self-esteem.

Enmeshment

Rather than abandonment, other narcissistic mothers are entangled. They rely on their children to meet their selfish needs. While a mother may appear to be self-sufficient, she may be emotionally dependent on her son and foster mutual dependency through adoring and controlling behavior. She may rely on her son to provide emotional support, listen to her, act as a companion, or take care of her physical needs and responsibilities. When he becomes an adult, she may look to him for guidance and management of her affairs and finances.

Above all, she manipulates and exploits her son to gain her attention, admiration, and satisfaction for her desires and needs. She instills feelings of love, importance, and value in him, thereby reinforcing his dependence. However, it is entirely at her discretion. As a result, her excessive involvement with her son can mask her toxic parenting. Typically, he pays a high price for his attempts at autonomy. He learns to prioritize her wishes and needs and feels obligated to do so due to her manipulation with anger, shame, guilt, self-pity, and martyrdom.

If he does not comply, she may use his failure to do so as a means of scolding and criticizing him. When this occurs, he feels let down or hurt by her. He does not feel good about himself or her, despite her attempts to reassure him that she loves and cherishes him. He becomes preoccupied with her needs to avoid conflict rather than focusing on his own needs and development. This can cause resentment and self-loathing. Over time, he may become emotionally detached from others and adopt an internal locus of control.

Triangulation

For a narcissist, marital relations are devoid of intimacy. As a result, a husband may avoid a narcissistic woman whenever possible. To compensate for this, and because she is emotionally dependent, she will "triangulate" (invite a third), whether it is work, a lover, an addiction, or her children. She may confide in or accompany her son. Children make excellent subjects for triangulation because they idolize their parents and are relatively easy to control.

It's even more difficult for a son if his father is absent, rages are violent, or suffers from a mental or substance abuse problem. The son may then seek solace in addiction or strengthen his bond with his mother to survive the discord in the home. He may develop low self-esteem, depression, and symptoms of PTSD.

If he feels burdened by excessive involvement or control from his mother, he will attempt to separate from her and establish autonomy. This can be difficult if there are no boundaries between them. In some cases, he will experience a narcissistic injury that can leave him feeling rejected, disillusioned, sad, and insecure—traits commonly seen in adult children of narcissistic parents. His mother can exploit his sensitivity to make her feel better about herself, reinforcing her dependency on him. In some cases, this can leave him with unbearable guilt and shame.

Issues of Seduction and "Oedipal" Nature

It can be more damaging when the mother is seductive and sexualizes her relationship with her son. Even without molestation, emotional incest may occur when mothers treat their sons inappropriately in language, appearance, and mannerisms. Some mothers will use their son's emotional state or intoxication to seduce him. They are skilled at manipulating and exploiting their narcissistic traits and their son's emotional vulnerability to satisfy their own needs.

In contrast, an adult child of a narcissist may feel "abandoned" by his mother if she is unavailable when needed, or neglectful, inconsistent, abusive, or distant in her love and attention. As a result, he may start to view his mother as worthless and resentful, and believe (often correctly) that she blames him for her shortcomings and problems. To compensate for feelings of abandonment, he might become involved with women who are unavailable or verbally abusive—as a way to fill the void in his life. This can lead to a cycle of emotional, physical, and psychological abuse.

Toxic shame, self-doubt, or guilt can also develop if he experiences abusive, neglectful, or inconsistent parenting. To avoid blame and shame, he will often avoid issues with his mother or stay silent about her issues. He may repress his feelings about staying connected with her and keeping her dependent on him. This leads to unrealistic expectations of himself and from others. He may use alcohol or drugs to blot out memories of bad interactions with his mother or magnify any positive ones. If an intimate partner abuses him, these same issues may develop later in life.

Envy and Command

To compensate for his mother's "abandonment" (even when it is not real), he may become jealous of others, especially his mother's attention toward them. He can feel abandoned, unloved, and unwanted when she doesn't attend to him or demand his attention. If she demands that he do something for her or gives commands rather than making requests, it becomes an issue of control—threatening his identity and independence.

To avoid abandonment and the fear that other people might hurt him emotionally or abandon him, he will try to control himself and others in an attempt to feel relief from these difficult emotions. He might blame himself, feel inadequate, and develop feelings of toxic shame. If he feels inadequate, it could stem from her lack of empathy or from her failure to pay attention to him when he was a child. She may neglect him as a way of avoiding commitment if she is emotionally unavailable—living vicariously through her son due to envy and jealousy rather than being there for him.

Due to his dysfunctional relationship with a narcissist, he may be hypercritical of other people, himself, bad parents, or the opposite sex. He may believe that others are just like his mother and can't be depended on or trusted. They will see through or manipulate him rather than support and affirm him in life.

The Harm Done to Narcissistic Mothers' Sons

As with their fathers, sons of narcissistic mothers do not feel loved for who they are but rather for what they can do to earn their parent's approval. If love is ever given, it is conditional. It is not founded on an appreciation for and acceptance of their son's unique, true self. The son's worth is determined by glorifying his parents' ideals and ego. This may include coercing him into a parent's preferred career and pressuring him to achieve success or the lifestyle his parents desire. They don't see their child's worth in what he can contribute to the world but rather how much attention, money, and status he can garner.

Codependency

Whether sons achieve material success or not, they risk growing up insecure and codependent. Their distinct identities have never been defended. Their sense of self-worth and self-esteem have been eroded by verbal abuse and an inability to love their authentic selves. They adapted to their mother's demands by suppressing their needs, feelings, and desires. This denial impairs their ability to engage in adult relationships. They struggle to identify and express their needs and emotions. Along with people-pleasing, they may self-sacrifice and feel undeserving. The father could not stand up to his wife to protect his children from her control and jabs; he also failed to set boundaries as a role model. As a result, a son may feel exploited, used, and resentful of women while not understanding how his mother failed to support or assimilate his needs.

Success or Failure

A narcissistic mother may see her son as a success, regardless of what he has done in life. Their narcissism can blind them to even the slightest hint of their child's weakness, insecurity, or failure. However, their children may also feel that they must overachieve to prove themselves worthy of parental approval—demanding perfection from themselves and others. Whereas sons of alcoholic fathers might work hard to succeed for themselves, sons with narcissistic mothers do it for their parent's approval rather than for what it will bring them. They may have a harder time feeling pride in themselves because they have been conditioned to believe those good things happen due to someone else's strength or success.

They don't develop healthy self-esteem or a sense of identity in themselves. They base their worth on not only their parents' approval but also the opinions of others. Whether rightly or wrongly, they will never admit it if something is wrong with them due to feelings of shame and guilt. Hidden beneath their perfectionism and driven personality is the fear of being found inadequate by others—especially their mother, no matter how successful they become.

Impatience

Narcissistic parents shape their children to be impatient and intolerant of others. When it comes time for change, their children feel unready and unwilling to adapt. They may act entitled and lack empathy when others don't meet their expectations.

Feeling Inadequate

The sons of narcissistic parents will never be able to understand themselves. Their mother's strong feelings of inadequacy and insecurity will remain a driving force in their lives. Their self-worth does not come from themselves; it comes from their parents' approval, material success, or achievements. If he doesn't achieve what his parents expect, he feels like a failure. He may never trust his own instincts and become an anxious, hostile, and volatile person.

Resentment

Due to his feelings of being manipulated and exploited, the son may develop a strong dislike for his mother, even if he remains close to her. This frequently extends to other females. In general, he will react to women in one of three ways: compliance, resistance, or rage. Some of these men will be aggressive and suspicious of women. Others have mastered the art of manipulation or passive-aggressive behavior. They are excessively accommodating, lie, or passively refuse simple requests from their partner as if they were their mother. Their hostile behavior may eventually cause their spouse to behave in the manner of their mother! Resentment and anxiety about intimacy may motivate them to be dishonest or unfaithful, especially if their father had extramarital affairs. The most common outcome is for them to be intolerant of others' feelings and needs or sexually unfaithful and abusive toward women.

Authority

They may grow up resistant to authority, even develop a defiant attitude despite their parents' long hours at work or busy schedules. This behavior can extend into their career choices, causing them to need little supervision and becoming micromanagers themselves—the opposite of what they experienced with their mother. Some have trouble following rules related to being organized or on time; others are insubordinate to supervisors and other authority figures. Others may feel unworthy unless they have the respect or admiration of others. They use charisma and charm to obtain their goals, whether from sex, power, prestige, money, or any other achievement-related motives. It may take a while for them to realize that they were conditioned to behave in a certain way by their narcissistic parents.

Physically Aggressive Behavior

Ego-oriented men will be prone to starting fights with others as they often fail to express their anger verbally. Their natural rage will often manifest physically when they have a chance to defend themselves or their ego against injury—due to disappointment, rejection, failure, or mockery. These men are often willing to do anything to achieve their mother's approval. Extremely competitive and ruthless in business plans, they may seek the approval of others through unethical behavior. Some may even pursue women as though it were a competition.

Making the Wrong Choices

Their behavior will be a derivative of their mother's personality, whether passive-aggressive or openly hostile and aggressive. If she was shy and timid, he might become shy and timid. If she was controlling or authoritarian, he might become controlling or authoritarian.

Most of these traits are unconscious and caused by his conditioning that his worth is based on obtaining approval from others. He may recognize some of these traits in himself as a result of this book, but his main concern will be finding a solution before it is too late to do so. Forgiveness from others and himself may take a long time, if it is ever achieved.

Daughters of Narcissists

Many young women grow up in their narcissistic mother's shadow, developing their dependence on an external source for achievement, success, or material gains. This may result from being made fun of by other children or adults who criticize them adversely, making them feel unworthy unless they excel physically or achieve success in some way (sacrificing themselves in the process).

Mothers are their daughters' first role models. When a narcissistic mother raises a daughter, her self-esteem and self-perception may be marred in three ways. First, she may develop similar traits that were encouraged by her mother, such as being self-centered and demanding. Second, she may develop traits to avoid the ones encouraged by her mother, such as being quiet and submissive to avoid criticism from others or criticism from herself for not living up to her mother's expectations. Third, she may feel unworthy due to low self-esteem or having only negative feedback for any success or accomplishment she has achieved—the opposite of narcissists who believe they are better than everyone else with delusions of grandeur.

Neglect

Many narcissistic mothers will not treat their daughters with empathy but continually criticize them. Some neglect may be due to strictness in controlling their daughters' activities, limiting what the daughter can do, or thoughtlessly blaming them for things that have nothing to do with them. The daughter's self-esteem may be lowered by having very little choice in what she does or where she goes, making her feel like her life is not her own. Narcissistic mothers are often controlling and intrusive, often wanting to know what their daughters are thinking and feeling before allowing them to do anything. They may control gifts from others, especially the father, to keep control over him and their relationship.

Lack of Boundaries

Narcissistic mothers hold no boundaries between themselves and their daughters. This can lead to a daughter's inability to form her own identity, boundaries, and self-esteem. She feels as if she is constantly on the defensive to avoid being criticized by her mother or peers (such as in school or at work) or is always giving in for acceptance from others. This can cause her to become dependent on external sources of validation, such as popularity in school or attracting someone who will give her the admiration that she needs.

This can cause the daughter to not have a sense of self, become distracted from her interests, and feel like people control her.

In turn, this can cause the daughter's self-esteem to deteriorate and can make it hard for her to form any close relationships or friendships. If there are siblings, jealousy and competition arise from a need for attention from the narcissistic mother.

Unrealistic Expectations

Narcissistic mothers have expectations for their daughters that are very unrealistic. Because of this, the daughter may not be able to obtain healthy self-esteem because she is not meeting her mother's expectations and thus not receiving validation from her mother that she is doing a good job. The daughter can even feel inadequate compared to her mother; thus, she may feel inferior or inadequate to all others. She may wonder why other people do not love her as much as they love her mother.

The most common expectation is regarding achievement in the educational or work field. The daughter may have been expected to be a star in school or become a doctor, lawyer, engineer, or other high-level professional. In turn, she can suffer from perfectionism because she feels that she has to keep up with her mother's high standards. Her mother may belittle her if she does not achieve the same level of education or work success that she herself did. She also may be told that if she does not achieve at the same level of success as her mother, she is a failure and is not living up to her potential.

Another expectation that narcissistic mothers can have for their daughters is physical appearance: the daughter should be thin, pretty, and popular, which all feed into each other. The daughter may become obsessed with her body and how she looks to others. She may become anorexic or bulimic, may exercise excessively, or develop other damaging behaviors to lose weight or keep it off. This can lead to low self-esteem when she cannot meet her idealized body. It can also lead her to be selfish in wanting whatever she wants, whether more food or another piece of clothing.

Parents encouraging their daughters to be popular can also make them care too much about what other people think in order to be popular. This can lead to a daughter being shallow and self-centered; thus, she can become more narcissistic herself.

The narcissistic mother may also act as if she knows everything. She may criticize her daughter for not knowing what she knows or feeling what she feels. This can cause the daughter's feelings to be invalidated or dismissed, which can cause her to stop sharing her emotions with others.

These unrealistic expectations can lead a daughter not to know herself. She may feel the need to be someone else to get her mother's approval and love, which can cause resentment between the two. She may also feel like she has to try harder to meet her mother's expectations. This can make her feel like an imposter or inferior and lazy.

Inability to Set Limits on the Narcissistic Mother

This unrealistic expectation by the narcissistic mother that the daughter should be the same way she is creates a sense of dependency. The daughter has no boundaries between herself and the narcissist, so she cannot depend on her self-worth or identity. Once the daughter leaves home, she may need to seek therapy to find herself and stop trying to be like her mother or going along with her mother's plans.

People-pleasing is another way the daughter may fail to limit the effects of her narcissistic mother. However, if the daughter learns to stop pleasing others at the expense of her own happiness, the focus can shift to pleasing herself, making it easier for her to form relationships and friendships. She may also learn to be self-critical in a healthy way to live up to her expectations of who she wants to be.

Being told that others are better than her or always being compared to others can lead a daughter to experience low self-esteem. She may think that if she is not as good as others, it will disappoint her mother. A daughter may also be told that she is why her mother is unhappy and not accepted or liked by others. She will feel immense guilt and be susceptible to numerous maternal manipulation tactics.

Throughout her life, the daughter may try to perform so well to prove that she cannot disappoint anyone else, whether a friend, a boyfriend, a teacher, an employer or another member of society. She may believe that it if she does not perform well, others will be upset with her. This can lead her to become depressed or anxious when she does not measure up to others' expectations.

Poor Communication

The daughter may not feel comfortable talking with her parents, especially if they raised her in a way that distanced her from them and fostered an unhealthy relationship. She also may fear the narcissist's temper and harsh criticism, so she avoids conflict with them rather than telling them how she feels.

The daughter may be afraid to tell her mother the truth. She may fear her mother's temper and resulting consequences, like yelling, or throwing something. This can create anxiety in the daughter, along with a tendency to hide the truth. This can cause her to withhold her true feelings or not let others in on what she is thinking and feeling.

The daughter may also be afraid that she will make a mistake if she speaks up. This can make her embarrassed and afraid to communicate with others. The daughter may use texting to communicate with friends and family members instead of speaking directly to them, isolating herself from others and causing her to avoid forming new relationships.

Accommodating Others

The daughter may go out of her way to accommodate her mother. She may be afraid that her mother will become angry if she does not get what she wants and that it will annoy her more if she argues with her. Her fear of disappointing her mother can cause her to detach from her own needs, thoughts, feelings, and opinions.

The daughter may also become a doormat for her mother to avoid conflict and disapproval or to gain acceptance. The daughter may feel guilty for wanting her own life and making her own choices.

Low Self-Esteem

If the daughter has a narcissistic parent, they will likely have low self-esteem because of their upbringing or way of life. Suppose the daughter is constantly criticized and never gets the chance to express her thoughts, feelings, opinions, or desires because it will upset others. This can cause her to believe that she is not good enough and does not measure up to others' expectations. She may also be told not to make others upset or angry, which will cause her to believe she is undeserving of others' love and affection.

If the daughter is compared to another person who has a more positive relationship with the mother, she will feel inadequate.

The daughter will likely feel that no one loves or cares about her if she does not have a loving relationship with her mother, and this can cause her to have low self-esteem and feel bad about herself.

Children with narcissistic parents cannot heal themselves from their past wounds if they are still being wounded because of their parents' behavior. Those who grew up with narcissistic mothers and now have children of their own might be able to regain a sense of self and find the strength to speak up for themselves. There are many resources available to help adults and children with narcissistic parents heal from the abusive nature of their upbringing.

CHAPTER 12: INHERITANCE

Children of narcissistic mothers are more likely to grow up to be narcissistic, or to have narcissistic traits. The children of narcissistic mothers are often narcissistic themselves because their mother is a selfish person without empathy and self-esteem.

Many of these children are narcissists because they were enslaved to the narcissistic mother's needs, desires, and emotions rather than their own. They live their lives by the rules and dictates of someone else. They feel empty inside because they have lost a sense of purpose and cannot develop their own identity as a person.

Not all children of narcissistic mothers become narcissists, but those who do frequently believe they are uniquely gifted in some way or have special talents that no one else has. They may think they always know what others need or want more than anyone else does. Often they feel entitled to things they do not need or deserve while projecting blame on others when things do not go well for them in life.

Many of these people are more than likely to live off the generosity of others because they believe they should get something for nothing. They may engage in illogical behaviors to manipulate others or win their favor. Such people usually have very shallow emotions and cannot process complex emotions like love, empathy, compassion, or sympathy. Many of these people never learn the difference between right and wrong because no one expects them to since they always get whatever they want in life due to the favoritism bestowed on them by their narcissistic mother.

The following are the signs that you may be repeating the pattern:

You have a difficult time dealing with criticism and rejection

You may have difficulty understanding that others can have different opinions than you and that people can be critical of you for things you do wrong. You may view your life as a movie, and everyone is part of the cast. You may feel entitled to special treatment and privileges, but you have difficulty handling things when times are difficult.

You don't understand why others don't treat you the way you think they should

You may have difficulty recognizing other people's needs because you always planned to be the most important person in the relationship. You may feel entitled and believe that you should be treated differently than others.

You believe that you are perfect

You may feel others are not as good as you, and you don't see how anyone else could be as good as you are, no matter what they do. You may have difficulty understanding why others do not agree with your point of view or why other people think or do things differently than you. You might see everyone around in terms of their own insatiable needs instead of everything having a purpose in your life. You may feel that you should get everything you want without earning it, and that no one should tell you what to do.

You don't value other people's needs

You may have difficulty being around people who expect special treatment from you. You believe other people's emotions are not as important as yours. People are just characters in your life movie. When their role is over, so is their importance.

You don't accept responsibility for your actions and behaviors

If someone points out that you did something wrong, you probably don't see it. You may try to avoid accepting responsibility by saying that you were unaware of what was going on or that someone else made you do it. You probably have trouble accepting negative feedback from others.

You have trouble reigning in your anger

When stuff doesn't go your way, you may feel out of control and compelled to act quickly to correct the situation, or you may explode.

You have a hard time seeing the big picture and making long-term plans

You always have a sense of urgency about everything, almost like it is a matter of life or death. The world is black and white with no shades of gray and no room for another person's point of view. People who disagree with you are presumed to be bad, incorrect, or self-centered.

You have difficulty accepting love and affection

You believe anyone who shows you love or affection is probably only trying to take advantage of you or use you, and this includes your family. You believe that people who love you are looking out for themselves and might not be as good as they are trying to make you feel they are. If someone loves you, they probably only want something from you. You may have a hard time seeing anyone's good intentions. Similarly, you may have difficulty expressing appreciation and gratitude to people who do things for you or show you love.

You have difficulty accepting compliments

When someone compliments you, you believe they are only being nice to you because they want something from you.

Your mood changes rapidly

If someone says something to upset you, it can put you in a bad mood for a long time which can be hard to get out of. You may try to avoid people who irritate you or make you feel upset and angry by staying home as much as possible or not going out at all. When someone else is upset, it makes you uncomfortable because it brings up your feelings of vulnerability and fear instead.

You have difficulty initiating activities or having fun

If you have difficulty initiating activities, this could be because you fear rejection if someone does not like what you are doing. If the outcome is not as good as you hoped, it is a big deal to you and could leave a lasting negative impression.

You have difficulty seeing the good in others or yourself

When someone does something nice for you, you often don't understand why, and assume their intentions must be bad. You may wonder why your family cares about you and worries about you when all you do is give them a hard time. You may feel that if someone cares about you or wants to be on your side, they are probably trying to hide something from you, or trying to get something from you.

These things can greatly affect children raised by narcissistic mothers when they become parents themselves. You may raise your child as your mother raised you without realizing it and neglect to give your child what they need, which can cause problems in the future. This can happen if you don't know how to care for yourself, cannot deal with your feelings, and cannot express yourself freely.

Things you may subconsciously do as a parent

- You spend too much time with your children, assuming they need to be emotionally controlled by you.

- You are too strict and critical with your children.

- You do not let your children do things that make them happy, making them anxious and depressed.

- You tend to raise your children the same way you were raised as a child.

- You may have a problem being assertive in front of your children.

- You might have a problem allowing your children to make their own decisions because you do not see them as capable of handling such things.

- You might have difficulty resolving conflicts or making decisions that do not accommodate everyone's concerns.

- You might not discuss family problems or issues that you are facing with your partner or children, which can cause problems in the future, especially when children are older and more independent.

- You might have a problem expressing your feelings in front of your children and telling them that you love them and care about them, which can also cause problems in the future.

- You may have difficulty seeing the good in others and giving up hope of having a happy family, making it harder to be a good parent.

- You might have difficulty asking for help from your partner or children because you do not want to bother them.

- You might fear that other people will harm your children or take advantage of them if you allow them to speak freely, which can make things worse for them in the future.

- You probably have trouble expressing yourself and you have difficulty letting go of negative ideas in your head.

- You don't find out if you are pregnant right away, which could cause health problems for your baby.

- You let your partner make all the decisions.

- You allow yourself to be controlled by your partner, making you feel like a failure as a parent.

You may not notice that many of these things are happening to you. It will take a lot of awareness and processing to change these behaviors and prevent them from happening again.

CHAPTER 13: RECOGNIZING THE INFLUENCE OF YOUR NARCISSISTIC MOTHER

Recognizing that your mother was/is abusive and selfish in her treatment of you is a big part of recovery. You may have to push yourself to confront the reality that you have lived with, denied, and minimized for decades. Some mothers are so abusive and cruel that we are in constant denial about the nature and extent of their abuse. The narcissist's child has a lot of work to do because most of her energy has gone into protecting herself from her mother's abuse.

Many adult children of narcissists find it difficult to acknowledge how their upbringing and childhood trauma has affected them due to grandiose false selves they constructed, and dissociation, which we talked about in earlier chapters. The trauma you experienced has been buried deep in your subconscious, and the grandiose false self, which was developed to protect you from the narcissistic assaults of your mother, has become your only means of protection. Your grandiose false self is protecting you from experiencing painful emotions.

If you have difficulty acknowledging the extent of your mother's problems and abuse, recognize that this difficulty comes from years of being traumatized by the narcissistic parent who was more concerned about her needs than yours. Your primary caretaker's abusive, selfish, and insensitive behavior toward you has caused you to dissociate from your feelings.

Many adult children of narcissists come to therapy and find out how much they have dissociated from their feelings. When they can connect with their emotions, they realize they had no idea how much damage the narcissistic parent had inflicted on them. They also confront their belief systems that created their false selves by invalidating real emotions in themselves and others and blaming others for all the pain in their lives.

The narcissistic mother is the number one cause of psychological, physical, and sexual abuse in a family.

If the narcissistic mother is not available or chooses to withdraw, the children must make sense of their experiences independently. The children can blame themselves for not staying in control and stopping her. They may blame themselves for being unable to leave or defend themselves against her maltreatment. Some children may even blame themselves for causing the abuse through their behavior toward the narcissist.

One way to avoid blaming yourself is to recognize that your mother's abuse was not your fault. It is normal and healthy to experience emotions such as anger, sadness, shame, and humiliation when raised by a toxic parent. Stop blaming yourself for not being able to make your mother happy, for your mother's treatment of you, and for her not being available when you needed her.

The narcissist's child has suffered greatly. The narcissistic mother thwarted her normal developmental needs, and she suffered from the denial of the love she needed from her parent. The narcissistic mother cannot love her children because she has become emotionally dead from using defense mechanisms that keep emotions at bay. Since the narcissist's child cannot get that love from her mother, she searches for it in other people.

Living with a narcissistic mother has long-term consequences. She will be with you in your adult relationships and family life because her traits and behaviors are ingrained in you and have become part of your personality and character. After you heal from her abuse, you will discover how much damage she has left on your life. You have internalized what she has taught you about yourself, love, relationships, sex, men and women, and the world around you. You must first recognize that you have been seriously injured in order to live a full and healthy life.

Willpower is not enough for recovery from the pathology that is your narcissistic mother and her effect on you. You need to use alternative methods to change your thoughts, emotions, and behaviors.

Acceptance

- Accept that your mother was/is not there for you emotionally.

- Accept that you have been deprived of love, validation, and nurturing your entire life.

- Accept that you are under the spell of a personality-disordered mother who does not have your best interests at heart.

- Accept that your mother will always be a selfish narcissist, and she is incapable of love.

- Acknowledge that the emotional damage she has done to you has affected everything in your life, including family, friends, career, finances, self-worth and self-confidence, partners and dating relationships, even physical health.

- Accept that you cannot change or fix her. You cannot change her or make her a better mother. You can only work on yourself to feel better about your life and relationships with other people.

- Recognize your efforts as the best you could do under the circumstances.

- Reach out for assistance from friends, family members, therapists, and support groups.

- Learn to live without your mother and be strong enough not to need her. If you must have her in your life, you can work through the relationship by healthy detachment.

You have to make enough changes in your life to heal from the abuse you have suffered. You can wallow in self-pity and negative thinking for only so long. The time has come for you to move on with life, have new experiences and relationships, and be all you can be as a survivor of narcissistic abuse.

How to Move Forward

- Become an independent person who does not need another person's approval or validation. You can do this by finding healthy people who like and admire you for yourself, not your relationship with your mother.

Not everyone needs another human being to feel good about themselves or complete. You can feel good about yourself and who you are.

- Get some hobbies that involve doing something other than what your mother wants you to do. These could include reading, meditating, walking, or biking.

- Improve yourself by taking care of your mind, body, and spirit.

- Exercise regularly to be fit and take care of your weight. This will help boost your self-esteem and confidence. Get a healthy body image to be happy with your appearance when facing the world in dating and social situations.

- Read novels, poetry, or books that will help you grow emotionally. Read other authors who write about the themes of abuse and recovery.

- Imagine what freedom would be like. Imagine how nice it would be to feel your emotions without reacting to them. Imagine seeing yourself in all your glory with no distortions made by your mother's opinion or behavior.

- Try to minimize contact with your mother. Try to have

her out of your life as much as possible until you feel better. This can be a painful process, so do your best to take care of yourself during this time.

- Help yourself by learning that you are a good person and worthy of love and acceptance.

- Avoid things or situations that trigger negative emotions in you. Look for something else to think about when these emotions come up. Avoid these triggers by staying busy with other things, doing different activities, or thinking about something neutral or positive. You can learn to create healthy coping mechanisms that will help reduce the impact of being abused by your mother on an ongoing basis.

- You can become more creative and productive than your mother will ever be.

- Recognize that your mother is not the only person in the world who can hurt you. You have to build a healthy sense of self-esteem and self-confidence, so you are no longer vulnerable to narcissistic abuse from others.

- You need to ward off narcissists or other abusers. You cannot be everyone's doormat or punching bag. Learn how to be assertive and do not allow anyone to use or hurt you in any way, including your mother.

- Learn to say no.

- You can be a strong and powerful person who can care for her own needs and feelings. You do not need to be a victim any longer.

- Recognize that nobody will come into your life and fix your problems for you, this is something you must do yourself.

- Learn how to be a healthy and assertive person without being too aggressive.

- Learn to take care of your needs and feelings. You will no longer be responsible for taking care of everyone else's needs and feelings all the time.

- Be assertive about your feelings.

- It is not healthy for you to be codependent and clingy with anyone, including a mother who does not have your best interests at heart. Healthy people do not need other people to feel good about themselves and their lives.

Even though you have been abused by your mother, and you have learned to be dependent on her approval of you as a person, there is hope for your recovery. You can learn to stand on your own two feet without needing any other person to feel good about yourself. You can learn how to be your own best friend rather than someone else's reflection of herself.

Realizing Your Childhood Is Not Your Fault

Many survivors of narcissistic parents blame themselves for their parents' abuse or neglect. They often feel that their mother caters to them and promises love, admiration, and support. Then the mother fails to keep her promises and is abusive or neglectful toward the child. The child feels that the abuse is deserved because they did something to upset the mother. They believe it is their fault and that they are not good enough for their mothers to be loving and kind. They feel shame, guilt, or embarrassment about their abuse, and their survival skills are weak because they are neglected and abused as a child.

Your mother's mistreatment was not your fault. Your mother is the one who should be ashamed of herself for abusing you and using you as a doormat or punching bag in her narcissistic world. It is not your fault that your mother mistreated you. She loves and needs to be seen by other people, and she will not love herself if others do not love her. No matter what she did to mistreat you, her behavior was her choice, and it was about her, not about you. You are a person with value and dignity who does not deserve abuse from anyone, including a mother who does not have your best interests at heart.

You deserve to be honored and respected as an individual. You are not an extension of your mother's needs or her ego. You are a person with value and worth. Your mother is not perfect, and she needs you as a loving friend and companion in her life, but she does not need to abuse you to get love or attention from you.

You have a right to have healthy boundaries – ones that are realistic and comfortable for the two of you. You have to honor yourself and know your worth without needing her to do anything for you.

Stop blaming yourself for the abuse and neglect you suffered as a child. You are a good person who deserves interaction with realistic, comfortable, and meaningful people. You deserve to be respected and honored as a person by everyone who knows you.

You cannot change the narcissistic mother, but you can change yourself and the way you live your life.

You can change your life, but you can't change the narcissist. It's impossible. It is like trying to put a square peg in a round hole; it just won't happen. So, why do survivors of narcissism often try to do this? They want their narcissistic mother to change because they are angry at her, and they want her to feel responsible for her bad behavior and what she has done to them in the past and their current lives.

If you love your mother, you probably feel angry at her and frustrated that you cannot change her. But it is better to be concerned than angry. You want her to get better, but that isn't going to happen until she sees a psychiatrist or therapist and works on her issues. Even then, it may not help because she may not want to get better anyway. After all, if she were better, then she would no longer feel special and superior.

You have to be real with yourself and move on from the narcissist in your life. Sometimes there's nothing to do but separate yourself from her.

CHAPTER 14: SETTING HEALTHY BOUNDARIES

Children of narcissistic mothers frequently feel oppressed by their mothers and powerless to resist them, even adults who were children when the narcissist was abusing them. This is because the narcissist, who is a control freak, has instilled in her children the dangerous message that their mother is omnipotent and omniscient.

Setting Boundaries and Priorities

A narcissist will attempt to control and manipulate their children long after they've left home. She will do everything in her power to make them dependent on her for love, money, and validation. She is an expert at gaslighting and guilt-tripping. But if you know how to set boundaries with a narcissist as an adult, you can protect yourself from her manipulations.

To establish boundaries with your narcissistic mother, first set priorities and decide what is important to you. This means identifying your values, goals, and rights, and making decisions based on your own needs, instead of the narcissist's.

Whether you were a child or an adult when she violated your boundaries, the process is the same.

The narcissist may have hurt you in one of two ways:

1. She did not love you

2. She did not support you

In either case, when you were a child, your self-worth was likely very low. This means that you might be hesitant to assert yourself at each stage of setting boundaries.

Ten Steps to Setting Healthy Boundaries with a Narcissistic Mother

1. Setting healthy boundaries means drawing a line. Decide what behaviors are unforgivable, intolerable, and that you are no longer willing to accept from your mother or anyone else. These may include verbal or physical abuse; controlling, manipulative behavior; lack of personal boundaries (stalking or intrusive behavior); abusive language; demeaning comments about your decisions for your life; emotional blackmail; neglect and abandonment—and more.

The narcissist may claim that you are overreacting but recognize that you have a right to protect yourself from the harm caused by her abusive behavior.

2. If a narcissist crosses your boundaries, you must take steps to reduce the risk of further abuse. You may choose to get as far away as possible from her, block her on social media, or keep vigilant about what she is doing.

3. If she breaks your boundaries and abuses you again, do not respond in kind or retaliate by attacking or insulting her. Remember that you are doing this for your protection. If you feel out of control, consider seeking professional help.

4. Narcissists can be very dangerous and unpredictable, so you must have a safety plan in place because no one can predict when she may become enraged and strike out at you again.

5. Once you have set boundaries and decided that you will not allow her abusive behavior anymore, you will feel empowered and restored. As you heal from a narcissistic mother, make a strong commitment to take better care of yourself.

6. Understand you were not responsible for her abuse or neglect. But now, as an adult, it is up to you to protect yourself by setting healthy boundaries.

7. Do not apologize for being abused or abandoned. It is also not necessary to talk about your abuse or neglect with her.

8. Narcissists can be very good at covering up their abusive behavior and making others believe that they are kind and caring people—and even the best parent in the world—so it will take constant vigilance on your part to protect yourself from further abuse.

9. Protect your friends and family by educating them about your mother's abusive behavior.

10. As you establish healthier boundaries with your mother and begin taking care of yourself, be sure to set healthy boundaries with others as well.

Good boundaries can prevent you from being an abused, disrespected child all your life.

Being Honest with Your Mother

It may have felt like your mother was perfect and infallible when you were a child. And as you got older, she probably told you that you were nothing but a disappointment to her.

If you are still living with or close to her, then it is time for you to tell her what she can and cannot do in your life.

By speaking honestly to her, you are showing her that you are not a child—you are of age and mature enough to make decisions for yourself, so if she disobeys your boundaries, you can walk away from the relationship without guilt about your own choices.

She may still try to control you by using emotional blackmail and threats. This is why it is important to maintain your boundaries at all times. Being honest with her about what you will and will not accept is sending the message that there is no room for manipulation or abuse in your life.

Here are some steps to take when telling your mother that you are no longer a child and will not be abused by her or anyone else anymore:

1. Do not talk to your mother while she is in the middle of a narcissistic rage or tantrum.

2. Make sure that you have time and privacy before confronting your mother.

3. If possible, have a witness present in case something goes wrong.

4. Explain to her that her behavior is abusive and dangerous and that you no longer want to be around it.

5. Be honest with yourself about what you can expect as you assert your boundaries—you may need to do some self-reflection and talk through things with a therapist and support group due to the intense emotions involved.

6. Remember that speaking the truth will always be right for you—no matter what she says or does.

7. Let her know that if she tries to control and abuse you again, you will walk away and never speak to her again.

8. Keep an eye out for more manipulation (i.e., she may try and make you feel guilty or tell you that she is suicidal or that there is something wrong with her. Do not believe it—she is doing this because she feels threatened your new boundaries.)

9. If the abuse continues after you have told her to stop, calmly walk away from the relationship in a way that does not cause a scene (this will take some planning ahead of time). Notify your loved ones of your plans and, if necessary, seek out a support group.

10. Be prepared for her to deny the abuse.

11. Remember that you are not the abuser. You do not need to apologize for standing up to your mother's abuse or neglect.

12. Keep an eye out for her attempts at manipulation or triangulation (i.e., bringing in other people to make you feel guilty or

prevent you from walking away). If this occurs, remind yourself that you are not abnormal for defending yourself against narcissistic abuse.

It is never too late to tell your mother that you are no longer a child and will not be abused by her or anyone else.

Getting Professional Help

If the her abuse continues after you have told your mother to stop, you may need to seek the support of a mental health professional who can help you both in your recovery process.

Working with a professional therapist is the best way to get through the emotional turmoil of narcissistic abuse—knowing that you have the support and skills to handle it on your own may be hard to accept at first, but it will make all the difference. Most therapists are very familiar with narcissistic abuse because they work with people who are in conflict or crisis all of the time.

Usually, there is a fee associated with therapy, but it will usually be worth the. You will want to research to find the right therapist for your situation.

Finding the Right Therapist

Once you have decided to get help from a therapist, you will want to find one that:

- Is licensed (some insurance will only cover certain types of treatment)

- Has experience with and knowledge about narcissistic abuse and trauma recovery

- Is willing to treat the abuse and neglect without blaming you for what happened

- Has experience dealing with toxic families, so knows how to set limits when necessary

- Accepts what was done to you and your needs

- Can explain what is happening in an easy-to-understand way

- Can help you understand and work through the emotions and thoughts involved in both the actual abuse and the recovery process.

- Is willing to help you learn how to set boundaries when needed (and will not blame either you or your mother for doing so).

- Can help with any other issues that might be triggered by things that happened in childhood (i.e., addiction, eating disorders, low self-esteem, etc.)

While you may have to try a few therapists before finding one that is right for you (and your family), it will be worth it in the end because they can help you manage the emotions and thoughts that are coming up from both the abuse in general and from the recovery process.

When working with a therapist, most of them will want to meet with you and your mother together for a few sessions to get a better idea of what is going on. They may also ask for permission to talk to others around you (i.e., coworkers, family members) about your situation.

If you feel that your therapy is not helping, then do not be afraid to seek another therapist.

CHAPTER 15: ESTABLISHING OBJECTIVES FOR THE HEALING PROCESS

Going through a recovery process is more like a marathon than a sprint. The first few months of healing are generally the hardest, but setting can help keep your momentum going throughout the process.

It's best to have realistic expectations. Recovering from narcissistic abuse will not happen overnight, and it may take many years before all the problems in your life are solved. You will likely experience many setbacks and disappointments along the way. However, if you are dedicated to working toward your goals, you will eventually move forward with your life in a healthier way.

How to set goals for your healing process:

1. Identify what you want to accomplish in your healing process, regardless of how long you think it will take.

2. Break this larger goal into steps and list them in a concise and organized manner.

1.

2.

3.

4.

5.

6.

7.

8.

---

3. Recognize that it is normal to have setbacks and know that you are resilient and capable of moving forward, regardless.

4. Identify personal strengths that have gotten you through this far in life and make plans to use them to your advantage while working on healing.

5. Set goals for activities or events over the next few months (such as how many appointments you will attend with the therapist or how many books on the topic you will read) to help create momentum for your healing process.

6. Recognize that life will not be perfect and that you will have more minor ups and downs in the process, but it's important to stay focused on your overall goal.

7. Identify people who can help you in your healing journey.

8. Practice saying an affirmation when you find yourself stepping back from your goals or falling into old patterns of thinking or behavior.

9. Discern your feelings and options appropriately.

10. Have faith that this goal will be achieved, and keep going!

Remember, you deserve a better life.

You can never be what your mother wants you to be, but you can be who you are, and that's good enough for you to heal and to be happy.

You will likely feel guilt and shame about your relationship with your mother. Childhood trauma will do this to you. Abuse of any kind will take a long time to heal, and that's perfectly fine. Remember that it is natural for recovery and growth to take time.

You deserve a better life. If you want to take your life back, you will have to learn how to feel safe in the world again. You might need some time to trust your mother, yourself, and others. However, taking risks is a part of the healing journey because it helps you progress toward recovery. Keep doing things that make you uncomfortable because growth only happens in the face of fear or uncertainty.

Being vulnerable with others will help you feel safer in this world. Remember that always being strong and never trusting anyone doesn't protect you from harm. If you open up to someone who isn't abusive, they can help you feel safe in the world. When people are close, they can support each other and love each other without being controlling. It is a natural way of relating that is healthy for everyone involved. And this kind of love is the type that heals.

Your mother wasn't capable of this kind of love. However, you can learn to be happy with people in your life and love them because that is a safe place for you. Even if this process takes time, it is worth the growth that comes with it. You may never be in a relationship, but you don't have to stay isolated and alone either – especially not when so many people can support you on your journey toward recovery. It is necessary to extend yourself to others and allow them to become acquainted with you. And once you feel sufficiently secure, you will be able to reach out and share your most intimate feelings with others.

As far as forgiving your mother goes, it can be helpful, but it isn't essential for your recovery. Forgiving your mother may make it easier to move on and be happy with yourself, but it is a choice that you get to make. Either way, it is perfectly fine to be angry. You'll need some time to recover from what she did to you, as well as regain your trust in people in general. However, keep in mind that anger only hurts the person who feels it, and there's no reason to hurt yourself when you don't have to.

Follow the Right Path to Achieve Happiness

You will only feel safe in the world by feeling connected to other people. And you can only feel connected to others if you are able to trust and open up to them. No one can know what the relationship between you and your mother was like unless you tell them. That's why it is good for recovery to be willing to talk about it.

Having support in recovery is important, but it is only one part of the process. Sometimes you will have to be strong and handle things on your own because no one else can do it for you. You will have to take the right risks in life and remember that there's a way out of any situation.

Recovering from abuse is a deeply personal process. No one can do it for you or make you do anything you don't want to do or feel ready to do yet. You discover the right path in your recovery process by making mistakes, facing them, and exploring better choices. This is the type of risk taking that you get to experience in therapy when you are willing to share everything with your therapist.

Facing reality is a key part of healing. Learning how to face reality and feel secure about it is essential for moving forward with your recovery.

If you stay true to yourself and take risks in your therapy, you will gain a better understanding of yourself. You will be happier in your relationships, with yourself, and in life itself, if you take these risks without being afraid of what might happen in the long run. That's why taking risks is necessary for healing.

CHAPTER 16: BREAKING THE CYCLE OF NARCISSISM

As we know, Abused children can subconsciously repeat the abusive behaviors their mothers taught them. This repetition keeps you in the cycle of violence. You may not recognize the pattern, but it is there.

When your childhood was affected by abuse from your narcissistic mother's actions, your mind may have developed an addiction to punishment or trauma as a child and teen.

It is important for all children abused by their mothers to break the cycle. Breaking the cycle stops the violence, and this has to happen for you to have peace in your life. You may have dealt with the vicious cycle your mother inflicted on you both as a child and as an adult. Breaking that cycle when you were a child was not possible because you did not have any other options at the time.

Breaking it as an adult is possible, although it can be quite difficult and frustrating. In this chapter, we will talk about breaking the pattern of abuse.

Remove Yourself From the Narcissist's Life

You will have to separate yourself from your abuser in order to recover from the losses you experienced in your childhood. You have to stop receiving her toxic messages that kept you in the cycle of violence by saying goodbye to her. You will now have to look after yourself and make your own decisions. In this way, you accept that you are now free from abuse and violence.

Rely on Yourself Instead of Others

Try adopting new behaviors to make things better in your life, even if they are difficult at first. Your new behaviors will help you stop the cycle once and for all. These new behaviors can be developed and changed over time, but they will have to start somewhere.

When you are actively trying to heal, it is most important that you stop relying on other people to make things better in your life. This may mean stopping some of these relationships or ending them if they are abusive. Develop a new life without relying on your abuser or anyone else.

Be careful not to reenact your abuse by attracting more narcissistic people into your life. Instead, you want to be accompanied by people who will help you reclaim your power and heal from the abuse you've suffered.

You will no longer need to rely on others for support and validation once you have broken the cycle of abuse. Then, the narcissist cannot control or manage your behavior anymore because you no longer need help from them. Your life becomes independent of them, and you will only be responsible for yourself again from this point forward.

It is important that before breaking the cycle of abuse, you learn how to handle it on your own by being self-reliant and relying on yourself instead of others for help. Learn how to be your own support system.

Self-reliance means that you will no longer need to rely on others. It will help you let go of those who do not help or support what is best for you in your life. Understand that you are responsible for your actions and what happens to you in life.

Self-reliance means learning how to manage yourself, break free from the cycle of abuse, and think for yourself instead of relying on others for validation. If people do not support your recovery or want to sabotage it for their own reasons, it is important to remove them from your life.

Let Go of the Victim Mentality

The cycle of abuse is perpetuated when you blame the narcissist for hurting you or anyone else she cares about. This idea keeps you stuck because you think you are responsible for making it right again.

But you can choose not to be abused by them, no matter what age or stage in life you are in now. You have a choice to stick with people who love and support whatever choices you make about your life, or to let them go if they do not support your growth and recovery from childhood abuse. Learn how to make healthier decisions about what makes you feel better and get out of your abusive relationships for good.

CHAPTER 17: TAKE CONTROL OF YOUR LIFE

The next step in your life is living it without letting anyone control your emotions, thoughts, or behavior. You can make healthier choices about your feelings, thoughts, and behaviors. Some examples of healthier choices are:

- Asking yourself what makes you feel better and making the decision to do these things.

- Stopping taking responsibility for anything the narcissist does when they hurt or manipulate other people's.

- Putting yourself in a supportive environment.

Stop Living Your Life for Others

You are now free to take responsibility for your feelings, thoughts, and behaviors. Nobody can do this for you.

It may have taken you a while to come to this realization. It was a lot more than just learning how to say no and call out other people's bad behavior. It was learning how to let go of your victim role and say no in a healthy way when someone hurts or manipulates your feelings.

Learning how to do this is the most empowering experience. You may feel scared the first time you do it, but when you can live your life by your own needs and emotions without feeling like a victim or being manipulated to take care of others and their feelings, you will find a new sense of happiness. It's a deep sense of peace that comes from knowing that you are not responsible for other people's feelings or behavior, and that they can't use them to manipulate you into taking care of them anymore.

The only way to take responsibility for your own emotions, thoughts, and actions is by giving up the responsibility for everyone else's as well. You don't have to do this all at once. You can take it in small steps over a long period. For instance, you may need to start with small things that make you feel better, like going back to school.

These are the next steps in your life. They are an opportunity for a new life in which you satisfy your needs, learn how to say no without hurting people, and live with no one but yourself controlling your thoughts or behavior.

Start Living for Yourself

Most people live their lives for others, but that is an unhealthy way to live. When you do that, you become the victims of other people's emotions, thoughts, and behavior.

Learn to be responsible for your own needs and emotions. Taking responsibility for your needs includes:

- Being able to face reality.

- Telling yourself how you feel and what you need to do.

- Taking care of your own needs in a way that makes you feel better by making healthy choices, with no one but yourself responsible for them.

- Not feeling guilty about taking care of your own needs.

Taking responsibility for your emotions, thoughts, and behaviors is a process that takes place over time. You can't change overnight, so do it in small steps. It's going to hurt a lot at first because people will react to protect themselves from losing control over you, but it's the only way to take control of your life.

You must learn to say no to people's bad behavior and to call out their bad behavior without feeling guilty or being manipulated into caring for them and their feelings. People who want you to feel guilty will try anything to keep controlling you, but they will stop trying if you learn how to protect yourself in a healthy way.

You are not a victim of your past, but you can't be free from the effects of it until you learn how to live your life for yourself by taking responsibility for it.

Learning how to say no and taking responsibility for your emotions, thoughts, and behaviors will give you the freedom you have been waiting for all these years. It may even give you a new chance at a happy family, if that's what you want.

This is probably the most critical process of your life because it will empower you to take control of your life and free you from other people's control.

Do not do this if:

- You are scared of being alone.

- You think this is a game and don't want to learn how to take responsibility for yourself and your needs.

- You want someone else to take control of your life without learning to control yourself first.

- You need someone else to take care of you.

- You want them to hurt as you do.

- You refuse to take responsibility for your own life and happiness.

Forgive Yourself and Start Over

You can't go back to the past and change what happened. Nothing you did can be undone.

But if you don't learn how to take responsibility for your thoughts and behaviors, you will always be a victim of your past, which means that others will have the ability to influence how you act and feel.

Forgiving oneself is the first step toward learning how to take control of your life. You are in control of your own success and happiness, so forgive yourself for what has happened in the past and take responsibility for your current emotions and thoughts in order to live your life as the successful, happy person you have always wanted to be.

If you don't forgive yourself, they will keep hurting you by taking advantage of your emotional needs and manipulating your feelings. You can't let them do that any longer if you want to take control of your life.

CONCLUSION

Narcissistic mothers play to your guilt. To keep you under their control, they do everything they can to make you feel guilty and responsible for their feelings of inadequacy. It is vital to understand their games. They do it to keep you feeling guilty and under their control. But you are not responsible for their failures and insecurities. You should not feel guilty if you want to change your life and create a happier future for yourself.

Stop making excuses for your mother's behavior. This causes you to continue playing the victim and allows them to manipulate your emotions against your best interests. Healing from a narcissistic mother involves dealing with feelings of abandonment, anger, sadness, guilt and inadequacy. It also involves identifying controlling people in your life and creating boundaries with them. Learn how to stop giving up your control over your life, emotions, and thoughts by stopping the people who hurt you from having power over you.

Healing is different for everyone. Some people can heal independently, while others need to enter therapy or join support groups. Healing takes time and patience, during which you may experience guilt, sadness, confusion, denial, anger, anxiety, and depression. Be patient with yourself; you may be triggered by a situation that reminds you of your childhood wounds.

There is no definite timeline for healing.

You deserve to be happy and to help yourself move forward from the pain of your past. This means you should no longer let your abuser make you feel ashamed about yourself or guilty for who you are. Begin taking steps towards self-love and acceptance. Above all, know that you are not alone, and that you deserve a happier life.